THE CLASSROOM

of

CONTENTMENT

Where You Learn That God Is Enough

Niki Lott

Christian Compositions
Niki Lott
(724) 510-9277
www.ChristianCompositions.com

ISBN: 978-0-578-54095-5

CONTENTS

PREFACE

I sat beside my husband on a swing overlooking the Smoky Mountains, and cried as if my heart would break. It was our first anniversary.

"If we don't have a baby by this time next year," I sobbed, "I don't think I can live."

He quietly tried to comfort me. Little did I know that ten more anniversaries would pass before I would hold our first baby in my arms. Nor did I know that while God would fill my arms and my heart, my womb would remain empty.

I was entering the classroom of contentment, not because I was wise enough to enroll, but because my loving and longsuffering heavenly Father saw my need and chose to place me there.

I won't pretend it has been easy, but the lessons I have learned have been invaluable. I am still a student, finding that each season of life brings new instruction, but also finding that the lessons the Lord has taught me thus far have given me hope and help in new areas I need to learn.

I hope to share some of these lessons with you. It is my desire to encourage you on your journey through this "classroom." There is a peace and joy that comes with true contentment that is worth all that is required to learn it.

My primary "classroom" was infertility. God may use a different area and means of instruction in your life - perhaps financial struggles, broken dreams, health difficulties, or an unexpected loss.

Whatever the setting of the classroom He chooses to place us in, the final question we must learn to answer is always the same: "Is God enough?"

I assure you that He is, but we must each learn the truth of that for ourselves and come to believe it from our hearts. With that question in mind, I invite you to join me in the classroom of contentment.

CONTENTMENT EXPLAINED

---❉---

INTRODUCTION

The Biblical Definition of Contentment

Consider the following statement, and try to finish it in your mind: "I would be happy/satisfied/content if…"

What is the first thing that filled "the blank" in the previous question? Was it money, a change in your family, relationships, church, status, appearance, or the fulfillment of some dream or ambition? Are you content now? If not, what do you think it would take to make you content? What does it even mean to truly be content?

Contentment is defined in *Strong's Concordance of the Bible* as "to avail, be satisfactory, be content, be enough, suffice, be sufficient."

Webster's 1828 Dictionary defines the word "content" as "literally, held, contained within limits; hence, quiet; not disturbed; having a mind at peace; easy; satisfied, so as not to repine, object, or oppose."

Take special note of the part of that definition that says, "quiet; having a mind at peace; satisfied, so as not to repine, object, or oppose."

Compare it to I Peter 3:4, "But let it be the hidden man of the heart, in that which is not corruptible, even the ornament of a meek and quiet spirit, which is in the sight of God of great price."

Contentment is a quiet satisfaction, but biblically it goes deeper than that. Before we can understand all that true contentment is, it would benefit us to learn what it is not.

According to the Bible, spiritual contentment cannot be based on the following:

Status

God does not want us to look at our lives and find contentment or satisfaction in some accolades or achievements. So much of what the world views as status has no value in God's economy. Fame, social acceptance, career advancements, personal or family recognition – none of these will satisfy our souls. In fact, many times, they feed our pride and leave us empty and hungering for more.

Stage of Life

When I was a girl, I remember that I couldn't wait to be a teenager. Then, I couldn't wait to be out of high school. Then, I couldn't wait until I was married. Then, I couldn't wait until I had children. Can anyone else relate?

Somehow we think that the *next thing* is *THE thing* that will make us perfectly happy or content; yet, when we reach that milestone, we realize we are quickly looking for something else.

If we are not careful, we will spend a great portion of our early life looking forward with longing, and the rest of our life looking backward and saying, *"If only I could go back to that time. I was happier then than I realized."*

As a young married woman, I got "stuck" in one of those stages of longing. I wanted children very much, but God did not give them to us immediately. In fact, God did not give them to us for 11 long years.

I so desperately wanted children and couldn't imagine how I could be content without them. The years of waiting were difficult ones in many ways, but much of this study comes from the lessons that God taught me during that time.

If we are looking for a relationship, a certain age, a "milestone," or something else to make us content, it will never happen. When we are struggling through something like infertility, an illness, loneliness, or even old age, it is very easy to think that if those "issues" were just resolved, we could be content. We may be tempted to think that we can never be content because of those things in our lives.

This is untrue. With Christ, we can be content in any circumstance at any stage of life.

Superficial Things

We live in a materialistic world, and especially in America, we find ourselves constantly bombarded by materialism and spoiled in so many ways that dissatisfaction almost seems like "the American way." It is easy to fall into the trap of thinking, "If I just had this…(car, house, hobby, trip, purse, wardrobe, bank account, etc.), I would be satisfied." The truth is, no matter how much or how little money you have you can be content or discontent (Eccl. 5:10).

It is easy to get caught up in the trap of appearances as well. We begin to think that if we lived in a certain neighborhood, or that if we could just achieve a certain weight, had different clothing, hair type, jewelry…the list could go on and on. We can easily get our eyes on the superficial, outward things to the point that we completely neglect or overlook the things that truly matter to God.

True contentment is not about *what* we possess outwardly, it is about *Who* we possess inwardly. Contentment is simply about satisfaction with God and His provision for me.

Spiritual contentment also will not be characterized by these attitudes or attributes:

1. It is not smug.

-Not conceited

Much of what this world perceives as contentment is really conceit. It is pride in what I have accomplished or accumulated. That is never God's idea of contentment. Paul said, "Not as though I had already attained, either were already perfect..." (Phil. 3:12).

Contentment is not self-important.

-Not complacent

Contentment with what we have and who we are in Christ is not a complacent, "I don't care," or "I'm good just the way I am" attitude either. The Apostle Paul was content, yet he said, "I press toward the mark of the prize of the high calling of God in Christ Jesus." (Phil. 3:14)

Contentment is not self-satisfied (Rev. 3:17)

2. It is not slothful.

Satisfaction with what God has already given us does not mean we are exempt from work or entitled to be negligent or lazy. We are to be good and faithful stewards of the things with which God has entrusted us (I Cor. 4:1-2; I Pet. 4:10). We are still to have spiritual goals and to strive for excellence in our spirits and our service for God.

There are unsaved and unspiritual people who can achieve some level of contentment. Charles Spurgeon once preached a message about contentment, and explained how some people reach a level of contentment with their positions or possessions because they are easygoing in personality, or maybe even because they have never been exposed to better things and don't know what they are missing. Sometimes it is because they have worked very hard and achieved their goals.

As desirable as contentment is, imagining that we are content apart from God is tragic. The rich man in Luke 12 exemplifies this type of worldly contentment. He was happy to have so much abundance that he needed bigger barns. His plan was to take his "ease, eat, drink, and be merry." The problem was that he gave no thought to God or eternity.

This study is about spiritual contentment - the type of contentment that is not an attribute we naturally possess, yet one that God desires every one of His children to learn. The Holy Spirit inspired Paul to write that he had learned to be content.

"Not that I speak in respect of want: for **I have learned**, in whatsoever state I am, therewith to be content. I know both how to be abased, and I know how to abound: every where and in all things **I am instructed** both to be full and to be hungry, both to abound and to suffer need. I can do all things through Christ which strengtheneth me." (Phil. 4:11-13, emphasis added)

Paul was instructed to be content. Paul said, "I have learned" this valuable lesson. What enabled him to rejoice in all things, to be content in all circumstances? If Paul had to learn these lessons, I'm certain that you and I need to as well!

Assignment:

Is there an area(s) where you find yourself struggling to be content? Take the time to write it down, and ask the Lord to teach you to be content.

Scripture Writing Challenge:

Scripture writing challenges will be included throughout this book as an optional way to copy and meditate on the verses in the study. You will need a separate journal or notebook to use for copying the Scriptures.

- ☐ I Pet. 3:4
- ☐ Eccl. 5:10
- ☐ Phil. 3:12, 14
- ☐ Rev. 3:17
- ☐ I Cor. 4:1-2
- ☐ I Pet. 4:10
- ☐ Lk. 12:19-21
- ☐ Phil. 4:11-13

LESSON 1

The Basis of Contentment

In this very first lesson we are going to learn the "Who" of contentment. It is a simple but profound lesson. The basis of contentment is a Person, the Lord Himself. Hebrews 13:5 says, "Let your conversation be without covetousness; and be content with such things as ye have: for he hath said, I will never leave thee nor forsake thee."

He says that we can be content with *what* we have because of *who* He is.

Think about this: What do you have that you cannot lose? Many of the things we look to for "contentment" - money, homes, relationships, health, security, loved ones, jobs – can be lost.

**If we are basing our contentment on temporal things,
then our contentment will be temporary at best.**

If we learn to base our contentment on eternal things, it can never be lost. We can rest in the knowledge that God has promised that He will never leave us.

Do you know the Lord? Are you satisfied with Him? Is God enough (Ps. 73:25-26)?

I struggled a great deal with this question when we were dealing with infertility. I remember my mom asking me, "Honey, is God enough?" while we were waiting for children.

I couldn't honestly answer it at that time, not the way I knew I should. It was a hard question for me, but I'm thankful she asked it. She wasn't trying to be unkind. I knew how fervently she prayed for us to have children if that were God's will. In confronting me with that question, she was trying to help me to learn that God was faithful, that He could be trusted, and that even when we do not receive the answers we hope for, He is still good, right, and sufficient.

If you know Christ as Savior:

- You have the assurance of His presence (Heb. 13:5).
- You have the assurance of His provision (Phil. 4:19).
- You have the assurance of His power (II Tim. 1:7; Jn. 1:12).
- You have the assurance of His peace (Jn. 14:27; Phil. 4:6-7).

If you know the Lord but are still struggling with this area of contentment, don't despair! Remember that Paul said he had "learned to be content." Contentment is something the Lord has to teach us. As we get in His Word, spend time with Him, and learn to truly know Him, we can learn true contentment. In fact, one of the primary roles of the Holy Spirit is that of teacher (Jn. 14:26). The question is, are we willing students?

My husband preaches a sermon on the difference in knowing God's works and knowing God's ways. If we base our contentment on what God does or doesn't do for us or give to us, we may be disappointed and confused when God doesn't work as we think He should. But if we seek to know God's ways – His character, His heart, and His mind – we can learn to trust Him and be content that He is choosing wisely on our behalf.

**"The secret is Christ in me,
not me in a different set of circumstances."**

–Elisabeth Elliott

Assignment:

Spend some time thinking about who God is. List some of His attributes.

Purpose to take time each day to thank and praise God for WHO He is, not just for what He has done or for something He has given you. Praise and thank Him for His love, His holiness, His grace, His mercy, and His longsuffering. If you are looking for ideas, take time to read the Psalms. Many of the psalms are thanksgiving and praise to God for His character. As we learn more about our Savior, and come to know Him better, we will find it easier to trust Him, to rest in His will for us, and to be content with His plan for our lives.

Scripture Writing Challenge

- [ ] Heb. 13:5
- [ ] Ps. 73:25-26
- [ ] Phil. 4:19
- [ ] II Tim. 1:7
- [ ] Jn. 1:12
- [ ] Jn. 14:26-27
- [ ] Phil. 4:6-7

LESSON 2

The Basics of Contentment

In this lesson, we are going to study the "what" of contentment (I Tim. 6:6-8; Lk. 3:13-14; Heb. 13:5; Mt. 6:24-34).

Hebrews 13:5 says we are to "…be content with such things as ye have…" It is put even more plainly and in more basic terms in I Timothy 6:8: "And having food and raiment let us be therewith content."

God says in that verse that there are two earthly basics with which we are to be content:

1. Food

2. Raiment (clothing)

That's pretty basic! God has promised to supply our needs. Are we willing to be content with what He has provided?

Read these two verses carefully:

(Psalm 23:1) "The Lord is my shepherd; I shall not want."

13

(Psalm 34:10) "The young lions do lack, and suffer hunger: but they that seek the Lord shall not want any good thing."

In both of these verses, the Bible says that we shall "not want." In the first example, it says that if the Lord is our Shepherd, we shall not want. In the second, it says that "they that seek the Lord shall not want any good thing."

There is an important distinction in *having* a "want", and *being* in "want." When we use the word "want," we usually mean a desire, a wish, or even a lust. When the Bible uses the word "want" in these instances, it means a lack or deficiency, to be destitute or in need. There is a big difference in a lack and a lust. God does not promise to give us every passing fancy or everything we may wish to have. He does assure us that He will meet our needs. Furthermore, the primary needs He promises to meet are spiritual needs, not physical ones.

Here is a tough question: *If you had nothing but the clothes you are wearing and food to eat, would you be content?* Do you think that is even possible?

I would like to think that the answer is yes for me, but the truth is that I have never had to live with only those basic necessities.

Here is another question: Are you content with the things you currently have?

Most of us have far more than what we need, yet we often complain and feel that we are deprived or do not have enough. Sadly, that is ingratitude.

Jesus deals with this in Matthew 6:24-34. Over and over He says, "Take no thought" – don't dwell on this, don't fret – about what you will eat or drink or wear. If God can clothe the grass and feed the sparrows, will He not care for you? Then He says, "O ye of little faith."

Oh me of little faith! How easy it is to worry and fret, to grumble and gripe, and to imagine that God isn't going to meet my needs. The truth is that when these cares are big to us, it is because our faith in God is small. God desires that we trust Him, and that we do it without fretting and without grumbling.

I love to read the story of George Müller. His willingness to trust God and to thank God in faith for what He had not yet provided are an inspiration to me. He lived a life of meager means by the world's standards, but a life of joyful faith and obedience to God. His greatest desire was to demonstrate by his life that God could and would provide for the needs of His people.

Consider this - Satan's first temptation of mankind in the Garden was for Eve to doubt God's Word, and the second was for her to be discontent with God's plan and provision. Eve fell for Satan's temptation.

When we are discontent, we are acting on disbelief, because God has promised that He will supply our needs. If we truly believe that God will keep His Word, then we should be grateful and content instead of grumbling and complaining.

The account of Eve is also a good reminder that we should be content, not only that we have food and raiment, but with the specific food and raiment God has provided "…such things as ye have." She had every tree of the garden that was good for food from which to eat, save one. Only one had God withheld from her, and that withholding was because of His love and mercy. Yet, focusing on the one thing she could not have instead of all the bounty God had given her opened her mind to temptation and led to her disobedience.

How often is that true of us! Instead of focusing our hearts on all the amazing and wonderful things God has provided for us, Satan turns our attention to that ONE THING we don't have and tempts us to be bitter, to be ungrateful, even to be disobedient to God in order to acquire that one thing.

Avoid the trap that snared Eve. How? By trusting the Lord, and choosing to be content with such things as we have.

Consider this testimony written by Fanny Crosby, the blind hymn writer whose beautiful words have inspired and encouraged so many in their Christian walk:

"As I grew older they told me I should never see the faces of friends, the flowers of the field, the blue of the skies, or the golden beauty of the stars.

When my dear mother knew that I was to be shut out from all the beauties of the natural world, she told me in my girl-hood that two of the world's greatest poets, Homer and Milton, were blind and that sometimes Providence deprived persons of some physical faculty in order that the spiritual insight might be more fully awake.

Soon I learned what other children possessed, but I made up my mind to store away a little jewel in my heart, which I called 'Content.' This has been the comfort of my whole life.

When I was eight years of age, I wrote these words:

> Oh, what a happy soul am I! Although I cannot see,
> I am resolved that in this world Contented I will be.
> How many blessings I enjoy that other people don't. To
> weep and sigh because I'm blind, I cannot, and I won't."

Assignment:

Answer these questions:

- Do I have food?
- Do I have clothing?

Stop today and take the time to thank God for your food and for your clothing. Each day this week, thank God for at least one material thing He has provided for you that exceeds these necessities. If you don't have it already, ask the Lord to help you develop an attitude of conscious gratitude. Be quick to give thanks to Him for His mercies and benefits, great and small.

Commit this verse to memory: "Blessed be the Lord, who daily loadeth us with benefits, even the God of our salvation. Selah." (Ps. 68:19)

Pause and meditate on this verse each day. What an amazing thing it is that the God who gives us eternal salvation also meets our daily needs!

Challenge Assignment:

Read a biography of George Müller. My personal favorite is *The Autobiography of George Müller.*

Scripture Writing Challenge

- ☐ I Tim. 6:6-8
- ☐ Lk. 3:13-14
- ☐ Ps. 23:1
- ☐ Ps. 34:10
- ☐ Ps. 68:19

Bonus Challenge:

- ☐ Mt. 6:24-34

LESSON 3

The Boundaries of Contentment

In this lesson, we learn the "where" of contentment (Phil. 4:4, 10-13, 19). Philippians 4:11 says that Paul had learned "...in whatsoever state I am, therewith to be content." The word "state" means "condition; circumstance." The boundaries set forth in this passage are very broad:

- In whatsoever state (condition; circumstance) I am
- Everywhere
- In all things

This section has been much harder for me to write than I imagined it would be. When I first began trying to transform this study into a book, my husband was a pastor in a small, rural community. We had been there for almost 13 years. I had developed this study over several years, primarily as a result of the personal soul-searching and Bible study I had done

19

throughout our years of infertility. I honestly felt I was content with my possessions and circumstances, and perhaps I was, but the Lord sure has a way of teaching us new lessons and challenging us to grow through different stages and seasons of our lives!

My plan was to write, edit, and finish this book while my kids were out of school last summer. While every season is busy, summer is usually a little less hectic for me as a home schooling mom; however, as we all know, our plans and God's plans aren't always in sync!

In April of last year, my husband told me that he believed God may be preparing to move us from the pastorate we were in. He wasn't sure exactly where or when, but he wanted me to know and to pray. I can't say that I was surprised. God had been dealing with my heart as well. After several weeks of prayer, both of us knew this was God's will.

Then came the many questions about "when?" and "what next?" followed by more prayer. To condense a very long story into just a few sentences, God confirmed in our hearts that He wanted us in an entirely new ministry, an evangelistic ministry with an emphasis on encouraging pastors, their families, and local churches. Within just a few weeks, *Refreshing Grace Ministries* was born.

I was very excited about God's direction in our lives, although sad about the inevitable goodbyes. God's grace was sufficient, and He amazed us each step of the way with His clear direction and abundant provision.

What I wasn't prepared for was how I would feel about sorting, packing, and storing most of my belongings. As I sold items and packed boxes, tears came to my eyes more often than I care to admit. I had to spend a great deal of time praying and asking the Lord to help me to be content with our new life and circumstances.

Early in our marriage, I had told the Lord and my husband that I never wanted to hinder him from doing anything God wanted to do. I wanted to be willing to live in any place, under any circumstances, and to do so gladly. I meant that, and I still do. That doesn't mean it wasn't hard and that it didn't require a fresh surrender.

Currently for me, that means temporarily living in someone else's house, traveling weekly, living out of suitcases a great deal of the time, and having the majority of my household goods in storage units. It also means getting to spend a huge amount of time with my husband and children, getting to travel and see many different parts of the country, enjoying hands-on home education and amazing field trips, meeting and ministering to wonderful people, and serving the Lord with my family. One more benefit? A lot less housework!

Contentment isn't a one-time lesson, and surrender isn't a one-time decision. As we grow in the Lord, and as life changes, we will find ourselves faced with new challenges and new choices. We have the opportunity to learn and the option to choose. I pray that we will learn to choose wisely.

You may be thinking, "How can I possibly be content in all circumstances, in all places, for all things? That's impossible!" And in our own strength, it is. Thankfully, the Holy Spirit answers our doubts and deficiencies in verse 13: "I can do all things through Christ which strengtheneth me."

We often use this verse to apply to different situations, but the context of the Scripture is that of contentment. We truly cannot be content without God's strength and help, but with His strength we can be content in any circumstance, in any place, and in all things.

This was no feat that Paul accomplished through his own will or goodness. It was the work of God in him. It was a lesson that he had learned by the grace and Spirit of God.

In Proverbs 30:8-9, we see these words:

"Remove far from me vanity and lies: give me neither poverty nor riches; feed me with food convenient for me: Lest I be full, and deny thee, and say, Who is the LORD? Or lest I be poor, and steal, and take the name of my God in vain."

Here we see the tendency of our human nature to be unable to deal with prosperity or poverty. When we have an abundance, we are tempted to be filled with pride and to feel that we don't need the Lord. When we are in a time of deprivation, we are tempted to disobey God and to blame Him for our troubles.

Paul had learned how to deal with both of these extremes. He states,

"I know both how to be abased, and I know how to abound: every where and in all things I am instructed both to be full and to be hungry, both to abound and to suffer need."

How can we get to the point where we can deal with abundance and need with the same grace and peace that sustained Paul?

The very next verse gives the answer:

"I can do all things through Christ which strengtheneth me."

Might I remind you that the Epistle to the Philippians was penned while Paul was in prison? Paul was content in a cell, and Eve was discontent in the Garden of Eden. Why? It wasn't because of their location or their circumstances. It all hinged on whose words they believed. Paul believed God and trusted Him. Eve believed Satan and doubted God.

THE CLASSROOM OF CONTENTMENT

A story that I heard as a teenager has often come back to my mind when I'm tempted to complain about my circumstances. It is a story of Corrie and Betsie ten Boom during the time they were imprisoned at Ravensbruck, a brutal concentration camp.

While there, Corrie and Betsie were placed in a barracks that was infested with fleas. Corrie was bemoaning their condition (and who can blame her!). Betsie began to pray that the Lord would show them how to live in such horrible circumstances. Suddenly, she remembered a Scripture they had read that morning. It was I Thessalonians 5:18, "In every thing give thanks: for this is the will of God in Christ Jesus concerning you."

Convinced this was the answer they sought from the Lord, she encouraged Corrie to join her in thanking God for every single thing about their barracks...including the fleas. It took some prodding to get Corrie to agree to that point, but Betsie reminded her, "It doesn't say 'in pleasant circumstances.' Fleas are part of this place where God has put us." And so, together, they thanked God for the fleas.

Despite the horrible conditions and the strict surveillance, they were able to conduct Bible studies and lead many to Christ in that room. For quite a while, they could not understand why the guards never entered the room to check on them, but one day they realized that it was because of the fleas. Corrie said, "My mind rushed back to our first hour in this place. I remembered Betsie's bowed head, remembered her thanks to God for creatures I could see no use for."

Corrie learned a lesson we would all benefit from – contentment and thankfulness aren't to be based on our circumstances. It is the will of God that we be thankful "in every thing."

Assignment 1:

Is there a place or a circumstance in which you are struggling to be content? Perhaps it is where you live, the time of life you are currently in, or a hardship you are currently experiencing. Write it down.

Ask the Lord to help you to learn to be content in that specific circumstance. When your heart seems to feel "I can't!" respond with Philippians 4:13, "I can do all things through Christ which strengtheneth me."

Truth: *Many times it is not that we cannot be content through Christ; it is that we will not. We have chosen in our hearts to be unthankful for a specific circumstance.*

Assignment 2:

Each day, thank God for the specific circumstance you are struggling with. Ask Him to teach you the lesson He would have you to learn through that specific "classroom" in your life. Praise Him for being with you in that circumstance.

Scripture Writing Challenge

- ☐ Phil. 4:4
- ☐ Phil. 4:10-13
- ☐ Phil. 4:18-19
- ☐ Pro. 30:8-9
- ☐ I Thes. 5:18

Discontentment Exposed

Niki Lott

LESSON 4

The Barrier to Contentment

The Source of Discontent

This is a hard lesson because it forces us to take a direct look at the root problem of discontentment. Although it is difficult to face, it is vitally important because we cannot overcome a problem or a sin until we are willing to realize what it truly is, confess it, and ask for God's help. If we get to that point, we can have victory.

As we study the Scripture we find that God does not say that when we are not content we are simply discontent, or unhappy. He doesn't say we are unfulfilled or dissatisfied. He says that when we are not content, it is because we are covetous.

Hebrews 13:5 says, "Let your conversation be without covetousness; and be content with such things as ye have: for he hath said, I will never leave thee, nor forsake thee."

I Timothy 6:6-10 addresses the need for godliness with contentment and describes that in verses 6-8. It then goes on to describe those who "will be rich," or who desire to be rich, and who love money and what it will give them. It says in verse 10, "...which while some coveted after, they have erred from the faith, and pierced themselves through with many sorrows."

God calls discontentment covetousness. Covetousness robs us of contentment. The Lord goes even deeper to be sure that we understand what the root sin of covetousness really is.

In Ephesians 5:5 we read, "For this ye know, that no whoremonger, nor unclean person, nor covetous man, who is an idolater, hath any inheritance in the kingdom of Christ and of God."

In Colossians 3:5 He says, "Mortify therefore your members which are upon the earth; fornication, uncleanness, inordinate affection, evil concupiscence, **and covetousness, which is idolatry:**" (Emphasis added.)

In both of these passages, we are instructed that covetousness is idolatry. This takes us right back to Lesson 1 and to a painful but vital truth. When we are not content with God's provision for us, it is because we love, trust, and desire something other than God. We are idolaters, perhaps not outwardly, but certainly in our hearts.

You may be thinking, "You have gone too far. I'm no idolater. I'm just not completely satisfied."

Finish this statement in your own heart, "I need Jesus and..."

If there is anything but a period after the word "Jesus" in that sentence, we still have a lot of learning to do. Perhaps there are some secret idols in our hearts. Are we willing to tear them down and lay them at the feet of the Lord Jesus Christ?

In Bible days (and still today) people made idols of wood, stone, gold and silver. There is nothing inherently sinful in those objects. They are "nothing." (I Cor. 8:4) The problem is when we elevate those things to a point of worship in our hearts; when we look to them as a source of help, or hope, or comfort, or salvation...or contentment.

Many of the things that become idols in our lives are not sinful in themselves. I found this to be a struggle in my own heart. Children are good! God says so. Desiring to have children is a natural thing. But if my desire for children brought me to a place that I was unwilling to trust God and was unhappy with God's plan for my life, then I had made that desire an idol in my life.

Read the Scriptures. Search them. There is no other answer.

Assignment:

Ask yourself if there is anything in your life that has become an idol. This can be defined as something you are depending on for help, comfort, hope, or contentment, or it can be something that is keeping you from being content with God, His plan and provision in your life. Name it. Write it down. If there is more than one, make a list. Be honest with yourself, and ask the Lord to reveal "secret idols" you may be unaware of.

If there is anything on that list, "tear it down" in your heart. Offer it to God as a sacrifice. Confess it as sin, and ask the Lord to teach you to worship, love, and serve Him alone.

Scripture Writing Challenge

☐   I Tim. 6:9-10
☐   Eph. 5:5
☐   Col. 3:5

The Symptoms of Discontent

When we become covetous, there are certain symptoms that will become evident in our lives over time. It is possible to have some of these symptoms without having all of them, but having any of them should alert us that we are in spiritual danger.

- *Cravings* (I Tim. 6:9-10; Josh. 7:21)

    When we are covetous, we have the wrong expectations and desires. Achan is one of the most tragic examples of someone who was covetous.

    God gave clear instructions about the spoiling of the city of Jericho. Achan saw some silver, some gold, and a beautiful garment. He was willing to disregard and disobey God in order to get what he thought he wanted. His covetous heart cost him and his family their lives.

    The problem wasn't that silver, gold, or beautiful clothing were wrong, but that Achan desired and loved those things more than he desired and loved God. God had forbidden those specific things at that specific time. God wasn't "holding out" on Achan. He was just asking Achan (and the children of Israel) to honor Him first.

    Doesn't He do the same for us? He asks us to bring Him our firstfruits, to honor Him with our substance – those things He has provided for us. Yet aren't we tempted, as Achan was, to hang on to things for ourselves? Don't we imagine that God is somehow "holding out" on us, keeping us from having what we really want or think we need?

    Eve fell for the same temptation, and we will as well if we are covetous.

- **Coldness** (I Tim. 6:9-10)

When we are covetous, our love for God will grow cold. As we have seen already, covetousness is characterized by having wrong desires, and we desire what we truly love. When our desires shift away from God, our love will also shift. "For where your treasure is, there will your heart be also." (Mt. 6:21)

When we do not get what we want, there is a great temptation to grow cold and hard toward God and others. We may not show it outwardly, at least not right away, but in our hearts it is easy to just "freeze up," perhaps even to get angry at God.

Ice numbs, and sometimes we prefer numbness to pain, but spiritual coldness is terribly dangerous. When we allow this coldness to creep into our hearts, we are damaging ourselves. Just as those who are dying of hypothermia don't often realize the seriousness of their condition until there is great damage or even death, so coldness of heart can do great damage without us always "feeling" the effects.

There was a period of time in my life when we had two adoptions fall through, one just after the other. The first one was hard, but it was through that first failure that we discovered the second opportunity, so I didn't grieve much over that one. There wasn't time. And it seemed that one door had closed to open another.

When that second opportunity was presented, things happened very quickly. The birth mother chose us, and her due date was only a month away. We excitedly began making preparations. Just a week before the baby was to be born, while we were finishing painting the nursery, we received the call that the birth mother had changed her mind. I couldn't even cry at first. I kept hoping it wasn't real. I felt like someone had punched me in the stomach, knocked all the air out of my lungs, and I couldn't breathe...for days, and even months.

The weeks passed, and I had to face the reality that there would be no baby. What would I do with all the things we had bought? The room we had prepared? The registry I had created? The emptiness in my heart?

To say I struggled would be an understatement. I was hurt and angry, and my response for a while was to just try to stop caring. I just didn't want a baby anymore. I would do my own thing. My heart felt like ice.

It's hard to even type those words. It makes me sad that I felt or responded that way. But I did. I'm thankful for a patient and loving God and for a patient and loving husband. They both helped me through that time, as did several other close friends and family members, but it wasn't without consequence. I know my coldness hurt my husband, myself, and others.

It was four more years before the Lord finally gave me a baby. When I look back over our years of infertility, my greatest regret is that I didn't trust the Lord more, and my greatest praise is that God was longsuffering with me when I wasn't with Him.

I don't share this to gain your pity, but rather to say that I can relate to the kind of pain that can lead to coldness. I implore you, don't get cold. It may seem your only option in the moment, but it isn't worth it. Share your hurts with the

Lord, and with others if you need to. It is not wrong to admit you are hurting. It is wrong to get angry at God. Trust Him. Don't run from Him, run to Him.

Covetousness always comes back to the heart, and our relationship with the Lord. Think of the question Jesus asked Peter three times: "Lovest thou me more than these?" (Jn. 21:15-17)

Do we love God more?

More than what?

More than anything. More than money. More than status. More than security. More than people. More than _____ (you fill in the blank). If there is anything we love and desire more than God, we need to ask the Lord to forgive us, and to help us to love Him most.

- *Carnality* (living for the things that please the flesh)

"And he said unto them, Take heed, and beware of covetousness: for a man's life consisteth not in the abundance of the things which he possesseth." (Lk. 12:15)

This symptom naturally follows the first two. If our desires are for what will satisfy our flesh and our hearts grow cold toward the Lord, our motives and actions are sure to follow. When we are covetous, rather than denying ourselves and living for Christ - for His glory, for His pleasure, for eternal rewards - we will live for the things that please and satisfy our flesh (even though that satisfaction is only temporary at best).

Jesus warns us to remember that life isn't about what we possess. No, rather it is about WHO we possess, and Who possesses us. Jesus followed that warning with the parable about the rich man who laid up much treasure but wasn't prepared for eternity. (Lk. 12:16-21) In very strong language, God calls this man a fool and again warns us:

"So is he that layeth up treasure for himself, and is not rich toward God." (Lk. 12:21)

What are we doing with what we accumulate on this earth, and why are we doing it? Are we taking all that God puts into our hands and using it for His glory, or just for our own gain and benefit?

- *Carelessness* (slothfulness)

"The desire of the slothful killeth him; for his hands refuse to labour. He coveteth greedily all the day long: but the righteous giveth and spareth not." (Pro. 21:25-26)

Covetous people are often lazy people who feel they are entitled, but have no desire to work for what they desire. It is interesting to note that the Bible doesn't warn of those who are rich, but of "they that will be rich," or those who desire to be rich. It is not money itself, but the love of money that is the root of all evil (I Tim. 6:8-10). Covetousness has nothing to do with how much or how little we have, but whether we are grateful and satisfied with what God has already given us.

As mentioned in the introduction to this study, spiritual contentment is not complacent or lazy. God commands and commends work. Proverbs has a great deal to say about the slothful person. We need to ask God to help us to have a content heart, but also a diligent character (Pro. 31:13). We should be willing to work and to be good stewards of what God has entrusted to our care.

There is one more thing to consider here: God often gives material blessings to those whom He can trust with them. Those stewards who labor for Him, who freely pass along His goodness to others, who consider all of their possessions to be His possessions, can be trusted. The Scripture above contrasts the covetous greed of the slothful with the generosity of the righteous: "…the righteous giveth and spareth not." A good test for our level of contentment vs. covetousness might be how willing we are to give of what we have to others. Are we greedy and stingy, or are we "cheerful givers"?

- *Comparing*

"For we dare not make ourselves of the number, or compare ourselves with some that commend themselves: but they measuring themselves by themselves, and comparing themselves among themselves, are not wise." (II Cor. 10:12)

As we have seen, at its root, comparison is dissatisfaction with God, but it often manifests itself as desiring what others have. In that sense, comparison is often both a cause and an effect of covetousness. When we begin comparing what we have with what others have, or what we perceive ourselves to be with what we perceive others to be, God says this is not wise. These comparisons and expectations can stimulate a covetous heart in us. However, if we are already covetous, we will find ourselves continuously comparing ourselves with others. Comparison can lead to many other sins, including ingratitude, anger, and envy.

- *Complaining*

"And when the people complained, it displeased the Lord: and the Lord heard it; and his anger was kindled..." (Num. 11:1a)

I encourage you to read Numbers 11. It is a sad account, but it is also a snapshot of a recurring theme with the children of Israel. They doubted God's ability to provide, yet even when He did provide, they weren't satisfied with what He gave them.

When we are covetous, we will complain about what we don't have rather than being grateful for what we do have. The children of Israel are a tragic example of this symptom of covetousness. We are told in the New Testament that God gave us the accounts of their sin to be examples for us so that we do not do the same things (I Cor. 10:1-12).

As Jesus said, we need to "take heed, and beware of covetousness." Look for it in your heart and life. If it is there, ask the Lord to help you to remove it. Love Him most. Look to Him as your source of contentment in every area of your life.

Assignment:

Do a "spiritual checkup." Begin with these verses: "Search me, O God, and know my heart: try me, and know my thoughts: And see if there be any wicked way in me, and lead me in the way everlasting." (Ps. 139:23-24).

Take this list of "symptoms" and ask the Lord if any of them are in your life. If so, mark it, confess it to the Lord, and ask for His help in forsaking it.

- ☐ *Cravings*

- ☐ *Coldness*

- ☐ *Carnality*

- ☐ *Carelessness*

- ☐ *Comparing*

- ☐ *Complaining*

Scripture Writing Challenge

- ☐ Josh. 7:21
- ☐ Mt. 6:21
- ☐ Jn. 21:15-17
- ☐ Lk. 12:15
- ☐ Pro. 21:25-26
- ☐ Pro. 31:13
- ☐ II Cor. 10:12
- ☐ Num. 11:1a
- ☐ Ps. 139:23-24

CONTENTMENT EXPERIENCED

Niki Lott

LESSON 5

The Bewilderment of Contentment

The Paradox

A paradox is "a tenet contrary to received opinion," or "a statement that is seemingly contrary or opposed to common sense, and yet is perhaps true" (*Merriam-Webster Dictionary*). The spiritual life is full of such paradoxes - truths that seem to be contradictory to the natural mind.

Here are a few examples:

- To live, we must die (Gal. 2:20).
- To be great, we must be servants (Mt. 20:26-27).
- When we are weak, then we are strong (II Cor. 12:10).
- To become wise, we must become as fools (I Cor. 3:18).
- To be first, we must be last (Mt. 20:16).

Spiritual contentment is one such paradox. While we are to find our contentment in the Lord, we discover that when we seek Him, our hunger for earthly things lessens. Our hunger and thirst for Him, His attributes, and His work in our life increases.

The Christian who is self-satisfied may appear content. The church of Laodicea described themselves in this way: "I am rich, and increased with goods, and have need of nothing…" (Rev. 3:17a). They were quite "content" with their condition.

God saw them as spiritually bankrupt. He said to them, "…and knowest not that thou art wretched, and miserable, and poor, and blind, and naked" (Rev. 3:17b).

The Christian who is seeking true contentment has a deep longing to grow in Christ, and to know Him better (Phil. 3:10).

Contentment is not a satisfaction in ourselves. It is a growing realization that I can find no satisfaction apart from Him and His perfect will.

 **Assignment:**

Can you think of any other spiritual paradoxes?

Do you believe what God says about these truths?

 **Scripture Writing Challenge**

- ☐ Gal. 2:20
- ☐ Mt. 20:26-27
- ☐ II Cor. 12:10
- ☐ I Cor. 3:18
- ☐ Mt. 20:16
- ☐ Phil. 3:10

The Passion

A Christian who is developing in godly contentment will have a passion to pursue Christ unlike any other. As we stop depending on carnal things to satisfy us, it will cause us to grow more and more dependent on Christ to fill our longings and meet our needs. Our love for God and the things that please Him will begin to replace our carnal desires.

These verses in the Psalms demonstrate this type of passion and desire for God: "As the hart panteth after the water brooks, so panteth my soul after thee, O God. My soul thirsteth for God, for the living God: when shall I come and appear before God?" (Ps. 42:1-2)

"O God, thou art my God; early will I seek thee: my soul thirsteth for thee, my flesh longeth for thee in a dry and thirsty land, where no water is; To see thy power and thy glory, so as I have seen thee in the sanctuary. Because thy loving-kindness is better than life, my lips shall praise thee." (Ps. 63:1-3)

This craving to know and please God more fully is seen throughout God's Word. It is often compared to hunger and thirst. Consider these words of Job: "Neither have I gone back from the commandment of his lips; I have esteemed the words of his mouth more than my necessary food." (Job 23:12) In this passage, as well as in the Psalms, we see that this passion becomes more important than physical needs.

We also see that it becomes more important than typical greed. Over and over, the Bible reminds us that God's Word and wisdom are more to be desired than gold and silver. While most of the human race covet temporal things, the child of God who learns contentment in things of this world will learn to desire spiritual and eternal things. (Ps. 19:7-10; Pro. 8:11)

Assignment:

How is your passion and desire for God?

Are you satisfied with where you are spiritually, or do you desire more?

Is there a specific area of your walk with the Lord where you have a strong desire to grow and to learn?

Based on what you have written here, take the time to pray specifically and fervently for these requests; don't forget to thank God!

Scripture Writing Challenge

☐ Ps. 42:1-2
☐ Ps. 63:1-3
☐ Job 23:12
☐ Ps. 19:7-10
☐ Pro. 8:11

The Parting (I Tim. 6:3-11)

In I Timothy 6, instruction is being given to a young preacher about discernment and direction in his life and ministry. While there is no doubt of the context of this passage, there is also a great deal of truth that we can learn about the principles of contentment and the dangers of covetousness.

God warns of those who drift from the "words of our Lord Jesus Christ" and "the doctrine which is according to godliness…" Some of the identifying characteristics of these people are pride, strife (arguing), envy, railings (evil speaking about others and especially God), and evil surmisings (evil and ugly suspicion of others). He goes on to say that they suppose that "gain is godliness." They have it backwards. God's view is found in verse 6: "But godliness with contentment is great gain."

Job's three friends made this mistake. While it is true that God had blessed Job materially, Job's personal and financial losses weren't due to some sin in his life. His friends had bought into the error that "gain is godliness."

There are many prosperity preachers today who are deceiving people with this same lie. God gives us a strong warning about these false teachers who "…through covetousness shall they with feigned words make merchandise of you: whose judgment now of a long time lingereth not, and their damnation slumbereth not." (II Pet. 2:1-3)

These people imagine that temporal gain – riches, money, possessions, status – are evidence of godliness. They use our own covetousness to prey on us, to introduce false doctrine, and to draw our hearts away from the Lord. God says, "from such withdraw thyself."

Covetousness is contagious and it corrupts. It is often subtle and seductive. Because of this, God cautions us to withdraw ourselves from these types of people. We're not to let them instruct us. We shouldn't expose ourselves to their influence. We don't need to imitate their lives or ministries. That may seem a little foreign, even hard, to our modern way of thinking, but God's Word is clear.

Spiritual contentment requires that we exercise spiritual discernment. It requires that we allow God to add the right qualities and attitudes to our lives. It requires that we allow Him to change our desires and our thinking. It also requires that we separate ourselves, not only from the attitudes of covetousness in our own hearts and lives, but from alliances with and the influence of those who would lead us into covetousness.

"They that will be rich…" – those who desire to be rich in the things of this world – "…fall into temptation and a snare, and into many foolish and hurtful lusts, which drown men in destruction and perdition. For the love of money is the root of all evil: which while some coveted after, they have erred from the faith, and pierced themselves through with many sorrows."

One of the traps that is most clearly identified by God, yet rarely recognized by us, is the love of money. It has brought down many great men and women. It has caused them to err in their faith, to fall into temptation, and to wreck their lives, their families, and their churches.

God clearly admonishes us to beware of covetousness. He warns us of its devastating effects in our lives. He tells us to discern and then to depart from those who are going down this path. He first says, "from such withdraw thyself" (I Tim. 6:5). He then goes on to say, "…flee these things…" (I Tim. 6:11)

We must remember that it is not enough to just separate from the company of those with these attitudes. We must search out and sever those attitudes from our own hearts. The greatest danger we face is not the temptation from without, but the temptation within.

If we are going to have "godliness with contentment," we must be willing to part from the attitudes and desires that breed discontentment. We must flee – run far and fast – from pride, envy, strife, suspicion, and the love of money and all the power, influence, and comfort we imagine that it will bring us. We must be willing to identify these attitudes in our hearts and ask for God's help in running far away from them.

47

Assignment:

Do you love money or the power and influence it can buy?

Have you been tempted to believe the lie that material blessings are proof of someone's spirituality?

Are you being influenced (through books, media, friendships, etc.) by those who do believe this type of thinking?

If yes, what are you going to do about it? How can you part from this thinking and influence in your life?

Scripture Writing Challenge

☐ I Tim. 6:3-6
☐ II Pet. 2:1-3

LESSON 6

The Beauty of Contentment

The Pursuit

"…and follow after righteousness, godliness, faith, love, patience, meekness." (I Tim. 6:11)

I'm so glad that God doesn't just tell us what to run *from* but also what to run *for*. He tells us as we flee the dangers of covetousness and false doctrine in our lives, we are free to pursue the godly qualities that will bring us true contentment, joy, and blessings in our lives. What are these qualities?

- **Righteousness - our *relationship* with God**
  (Phil. 3:9; Tit. 3:5; Isa. 64:6; Tit. 2:12)

  Our righteousness is only and always a result of the work of God in our lives, and the relationship and fellowship we have with Him.

  Righteousness is placed inwardly upon us by God at salvation (II Tim. 3:16; Rom. 4:2-6, 20-25; Isa. 61:10; Rom. 10:3-13, 17; Gal. 2:20-21; Phil. 3:9).

  We have no righteousness of our own, and yet we can be righteous through faith in Jesus Christ. The Bible says that when we call upon the Lord in faith, this righteousness is "imputed" – reckoned, accounted –

to us. His righteousness is placed on our account. Our sin is placed on His account. What an amazing, beautiful, and powerful truth!

Righteousness does not procure salvation; it is the product of salvation. (Isa. 64:6)

It is not a reason we obtain salvation; it is the result of obtaining salvation.

It is placed upon us at salvation by God's grace through faith. (Eph. 2:8-10)

Righteousness is produced in us by God after salvation.

How can we have righteousness, not only positionally, but practically in our daily lives? God produces the fruit of righteousness in our lives:

- *Through faith in God's Word.* (Phil. 3:9; Rom. 1:17; 10:17)
  Righteousness comes by faith, and must be carried out by faith.

- *Through yielded obedience to God's Word.* (Rom. 8:4-6; Rom. 6:9-19)

Righteousness should be pursued outwardly for God after salvation. (I Tim. 6:11; II Tim. 2:22)

God has given us everything we need to live outwardly what He has made us inwardly. Pursuing a life of righteousness brings glory to God.

Throughout the Bible, righteousness is compared to clothing – a breastplate, a robe, a priest's garment (Job 29:14; Ps. 132:9; Isa. 59:17; 61:10; Eph. 6:14). It is to be a visible covering in our lives. It guards our lives and glorifies the Lord.

Ephesians 4 speaks of the difference in the "old man" and the "new man." It describes the contrast between our life of unrighteousness before Christ and the life of righteousness we should live in Christ. It teaches us the characteristics of this "new man, which after God is created in righteousness and true holiness." Verses 25-32 go on to list many of the things that we are to "put off" and "put on" as the children of righteousness:

- We are to "put away" lying and speak truth.
- We are to be angry and sin not.
- We are not to steal, but instead to work that we may give to those in need.
- We are not to let corrupt communication proceed out of our mouth, but instead are to speak words that are good and filled with grace.
- We are not to grieve the Holy Spirit.
- We are to put away bitterness, wrath, anger, clamour, evil speaking, and malice, and instead we are to be kind, tenderhearted, and forgiving.

What kind of "clothing" are we putting on today? As God's children, He wants us to live and behave in a way that demonstrates His nature, His mind, and His glory. He desires that we be right with Him and do right to others. Through His grace and power, we can live in a way that is righteous and holy.

Are we hungry and thirsty for righteousness? Are we pursuing righteousness with the same type of intensity that we would pursue food when we're hungry, a drink when we're thirsty, or riches when we're covetous? God promises that those who hunger and thirst for righteousness will be filled. (Mt. 5:6)

Assignment:

When did you receive the righteousness of God (when did you trust Christ as your Savior)?

Are you actively seeking to live a righteous and holy life, both inwardly and outwardly?

Are there any areas where you could "put on" the garments of righteousness?

If there is unrighteousness in our lives, we can claim the promise found in I John 1:9. Write that promise here:

Scripture Writing Challenge

- ☐ I Tim. 6:11
- ☐ Phil. 3:9
- ☐ Tit. 3:5
- ☐ Isa. 64:6
- ☐ Tit. 2:12
- ☐ II Tim. 3:16
- ☐ Isa. 61:10
- ☐ Gal. 2:20-21

- ☐ Eph. 2:8-10
- ☐ Rom. 1:17
- ☐ II Tim. 2:22
- ☐ Job 29:14
- ☐ Ps. 132:9
- ☐ Mt. 5:6
- ☐ Isa. 59:17
- ☐ Eph. 6:14

Bonus Challenge:

- ☐ Rom. 10:3-13, 17
- ☐ Rom. 8:4-6
- ☐ Rom. 6:9-19
- ☐ Eph. 4:25-32

- **Godliness – Our *reflection* of God** (I Tim. 2:10; Tit. 2:12)

Godliness is our inward devotion toward God that expresses itself in our outward deeds. It is a piety of heart that is reflected in the purity of our lives. It is the fullness of God's Spirit flowing out in good works. It is the light that shines before men in such a way that while they see our good works, they glorify our great God.

In order to live in a godly way, we must deny "ungodliness and worldly lusts." As we have already learned, there is always a parting of the ways when we determine to follow Christ. We cannot live godly and live worldly at the same time. We must choose to flee one in order to follow the other. We must learn to die to self, to allow Christ to live through us, if we are to be like Him. (II Cor. 5:15; Rom. 6:10-11; Gal. 2:20)

Titus speaks of living godly "in this present world." It is easy to think that we cannot truly live a godly life in the corrupt culture in which we live. It is easy to believe that we must be like the world in order to win the world. However, neither of those thoughts are true.

The grace of God that extends salvation to us also enables us to over-come sin and empowers and educates us to "live soberly, righteously, and godly in this present world."

We have heard the question, "Can others see Jesus in you?" We should seek to answer it honestly.

Assignment:

Would your family, friends, and neighbors describe you as a godly person – not religious, but godly?

Are there any areas of "ungodliness and worldly lusts" that need to be denied in your life?

What are some of the ways that we can learn to have and display the mind of Christ (Phil. 2:1-11)? Try to name at least five.

Scripture Writing Challenge

☐ I Tim. 2:10
☐ II Cor. 5:15
☐ Rom. 6:10-11 (*omit if already done in previous bonus section)

Bonus Challenge:

☐ Phil. 2:1-11

- **Faith – Our *reliance* upon God** (Pro. 3:5-7; Heb. 10:38; 11:1-6)

The life of contentment must be lived by faith. The Christian life begins, continues, and ends with faith. This is not just a generic belief. It is very clear and specific.

- **Genuine faith is clear in its object.**

  The world likes the idea of faith. "Just believe" and "have faith" are popular mantras, but have little meaning. Faith must have an object. "Just believe" in what or whom? For the Christian, we must be continually aware that it is not enough to just "have faith." We are clearly instructed and often reminded to have faith in God. (Mk. 11:22)

  We are tempted to have faith in ourselves and are continuously encouraged to do so by the world. We must counter that temptation with the many instructions God's Word gives us. Scriptural admonitions like "...lean not unto thine own understanding..." and "He that trusteth in his own heart is a fool" should be often brought to our remembrance.

  We can also be tempted to have faith in this world, in power, in money, and in so many other unstable things. We must be careful to keep our faith firmly fixed on the right object – our unchanging Savior and His perfect Word. (Rom. 10:17)

- **Genuine faith is clear in its obedience.**

  True faith demonstrates itself in obedience to the Word of God. James reminds us that if we hear the Word of God and imagine we believe it but refuse to obey it, we are deceiving ourselves. (Jas. 1:22) We need to "follow after" obedient faith.

Assignment:

Consider the object and obedience of your faith. Is your faith founded on God and His Word?

What if the Word of God contradicts popular opinion or your own thinking? Is there an area in your life that this is true? How are you responding?

Are you actively, intentionally obeying the Word of God?

Scripture Writing Challenge

- ☐ Pro. 3:5-7
- ☐ Heb. 10:38
- ☐ Mk. 11:22
- ☐ Rom. 10:17
- ☐ Jas. 1:22

Bonus Challenge:

- ☐ Heb. 11:1-6

- **Love – Our *revelation* of God to others** (I Jn. 3:18; I Cor. 13)

We could spend much time studying what biblical love is and what it isn't. Our world is so confused about love. Sadly, many times, even as children of God, we are also confused about love.

The love we need and should want to follow in our lives is the love of Christ. It is by love that the world will know that we are truly His disciples (Jn. 13:35). If we are to demonstrate this type of love, we must know and understand it. The following thoughts are by no means an exhaustive study of biblical love, but they can help give us a basic understanding and some encouraging reminders.

Christ's love commences. Our love responds.

"We love Him, because He first loved us." (I Jn. 4:19) We should never get over the wonder of knowing that God loves us. Just as He loved us first, even when we were His enemies, so we should love others (Mt. 5:44; Rom. 5:10). We should be willing to initiate love.

Christ's love commits. Our love rests.

There is an amazing comfort and peace in the knowledge that God's love for us is unshakable. There is nothing that can separate us from the love of God. (Rom. 8:35-39; Zeph. 3:17) As we learn His love and become more like Him, we are able to offer this same type of steadfast love to others. (I Cor. 3:4-8)

Christ's love conquers. Our love rejoices.

No matter our circumstances, because of the love of Christ we are conquerors. (Rom. 8:37; I Cor. 13:8) This gives us a reason to rejoice! His love allows us to conquer fear (I Jn. 4:18), and to conquer sin.

There seems to be a great deal of confusion about this particular point. While it is true that Christ loved us "while we were yet sinners," He loves us enough to free us from that sin if we will turn to Him. His love never approves of sin in our lives. He loves us enough to provide a way of escape from sin, not an excuse to remain in it.

The love that we can share with others through Christ also has the power to conquer. It has the power to overcome many obstacles. Genuine, Christlike love cares about people who are sinners (just like we are), but doesn't condone sin. Charity does not rejoice in iniquity or sin, but rather rejoices in truth. (I Cor. 13:6)

Christ's love constrains. Our love relinquishes.

The Bible says that it is His love that constrains us. (II Cor. 5:14) It compels us and holds us in. It sometimes stops us from doing those things that would go outside the constraints of His love. If we love Him, our love surrenders to that constraint. It is willingly "held in," just as a bride and groom willingly vow to be faithful to one another as long as they live. Their love is gladly constrained to be focused on one single person and object. When we love Christ as we should, we gladly relinquish our love for the world and the things in it. (I Jn. 2:15) This love for Him also teaches us to relinquish our selfish desires and rights in order to love those around us.

Christ's love communicates. Our love reveals.

Christ communicates His love to us through His Word and His Spirit. (Jn. 17:26; Eph. 4:15) He demonstrated His love by His death for us (Rom. 5:8; I Jn. 4:10). We reveal our love to Him and to others by what we say, but even more by what we do. As I John 3:18 says, "My little children, let us not love in word, neither in tongue; but in deed and in truth." It is important that our actions toward God and toward others are consistent with our words. We need to tell others of God's love for them and of our love for them. We need to then show others by our actions and attitudes that our words are genuine. Our words, our wisdom, and even our works are meaningless if they are not motivated by charity. (I Cor. 13:1-3) God wants us to shed His love abroad freely to others and to love them as He has loved us. (Rom. 5:5; I Cor. 13; Jn. 13:34-35; 15:12, 17; I Thes. 3:12)

Christ's love commands. Our love reacts.

"If ye love me, keep my commandments." (Jn. 14:15)

These seven brief words concisely and completely summarize how we should react to His love. To react is to respond by action. Because He loves us, He instructs and commands us. Our keeping of His commandments is not about somehow earning His love; it is evidence of our love. It is not a means of meriting His love, but of measuring ours.

How do we know if we love God? It is not by how we feel or by what we say, but by whether or not we obey His words. "For this is the love of God, that we keep his commandments: and his commandments are not grievous." (I Jn. 5:3)

The commandment to love God with all that we are is the greatest commandment and should be the greatest aim of our lives. Our love for God should surpass and supersede every other love in our lives. It must be greater than our love for self, our love for our friends, and even our love for our families. This love for God should be the motivating factor in everything we do and say.

In every virtue and fruit God desires to develop in our lives, He enables us to grow outwardly in our attitudes and actions toward others as we grow inwardly in our walk with Him. Love is no different.

How can we best love those around us? By first loving Him that is within us.

As our love for God grows and matures, it will be evidenced and expressed in our desire to be in His presence, our diligence to keep His commandments, and our deeds before Him and to others.

This love will flow in spiritual order:

1. It will commence in our spirits as we fellowship with Him.

2. It will continue in our souls as we decide to fully commit to Him.

3. It will be completed in our bodies as we follow His commandments and meet the needs of others.

An obedient walk with the Lord will allow Him to perfect His love in us, and that love will be evident to those who are around us. (I Jn. 2:3-5, 15-17; 3:16-18; 4:7-12, 16-21; 5:2-3)

Assignment:

Read I Corinthians 13. Wherever the word "charity" is used, insert your name. This isn't to try to change the Scripture but to help us to realize the personal attitudes and actions that God wants to develop in our lives as we love Him and others. Are there any specific areas where God needs to teach you to love as He does?

Challenge Assignment:

Find and read the book, *If*, by Amy Carmichael.

If you do not order a copy to read, search for quotes from it online. Write down at least three quotes that cause you to think about how you can have a more Christlike love.

Scripture Writing Challenge

- ☐ I Jn. 3:16-18
- ☐ Zeph. 3:17
- ☐ II Cor. 5:14
- ☐ I Jn. 2:3-5, 15-17
- ☐ Jn. 17:26
- ☐ Eph. 4:15

- ☐ Rom. 5:5, 8
- ☐ Jn. 13:34-35
- ☐ Jn. 15:12, 17
- ☐ I Thes. 3:2
- ☐ Jn. 14:15
- ☐ I Jn. 5:2-3

Bonus Challenge:

- ☐ Rom. 8:35-39
- ☐ I Jn. 4:7-12; 16-21
- ☐ I Cor. 13

- **Patience – Our *realization* that God's will is perfect**

Patience comes as a result of the testing of our faith. Patience is a work God does in our lives to mature and complete us. Patience is quietly, calmly enduring hardship and trials. It is being willing to wait cheerfully, without complaint, for God's timing. It is gentle forbearance with those who are not so gentle or forbearing toward us. It is steadfast continuance, despite opposition or even persecution.

Just as we must let God's peace rule in our lives, so we must let His patience work in our lives. (Jas. 1:2-4) As we do so, we find that the fiery trials He permits are the very things He has chosen to refine and purify us so that we can more fully reflect His working and glory in our lives. (I Pet. 4:12-13)

Most of us know that we need patience, but we tend to avoid or resist the work of patience in our lives because it is often a painful process. This passage (I Tim. 6:11) teaches us to follow after patience. Desire it. Seek it. Allow it.

When God works patience in our lives, we find on the other side that it is a beautiful thing. Just as you may dread a needed surgery but are thankful for the results when the pain and healing are complete, so we often postpone the work of patience, only and always to our own detriment.

I encourage you to "let patience have her perfect work." Pursue it. It is one of the key factors to finding true contentment in your life.

Assignment:

In what areas is God testing your faith?

Are you letting patience work? Sometimes we fight the process. Can you identify any ways that you may be keeping patience from having her perfect work in your life?

Many times when we don't "let patience have her perfect work," covetousness can creep in. Read Psalm 37. What are some of the dangers or demonstrations of resisting the work of patience?

Scripture Writing Challenge

- [ ] Jas. 1:2-4
- [ ] I Pet. 4:12-13
- [ ] Ps. 37:7

- **Meekness - our *reaction* to God and others** (II Tim. 2:24-26; I Pet. 3:4; Tit. 3:2; Eph. 4:2)

Meekness is humble, yielded, obedient, and content. It is a defining quality of someone who has yielded control in their life to the Spirit of God and has found Him to be the source of their confidence and their contentment.

Paul said, "I know both how to be abased, and I know how to abound..." (Phil. 4:12) In II Cor. 10:1, he said, "Now I Paul myself beseech you by the meekness and gentleness of Christ, who in presence am base among you..."

Paul had learned the humility required for meekness and contentment. This quality, so perfectly exemplified in our Lord Jesus, is greatly underestimated in our world today. Meekness is one of our greatest needs.

Why should we want to follow after meekness?

- *Because meek people have yielded control of themselves to God, He often entrusts them with leadership. (Num. 12:3)*
- *Because meek people have yielded their desires to God, He promises they will be satisfied. (Ps. 22:26)*
- *Because meek people view themselves honestly through the mirror of God's Word, they have no illusions about themselves and do not depend on themselves for guidance, so God promises to lead them. (Ps. 25:9)*
- *Because meek people are willing to admit their utter dependence on God and their lack of wisdom, He promises to teach them. (Ps. 25:9)*
- *Because meek people have relinquished their rights on this earth to God, He promises them an inheritance and peace. (Ps. 37:11; Mt. 5:5)*
- *Because meek people are not insistent on living for their own pleasure, God promises to increase their joy. (Isa. 29:19)*

One of the sweetest yet most rarely talked about attributes of our Lord Jesus Christ is His meekness. He who could rightfully demand the multitudes to worship on their faces came to this earth "meek and lowly in heart." (Mt. 11:29; 21:5; II Cor. 10:1)

He was humble. He made Himself of no reputation. He was obedient. He was a servant. (Phil. 2:3-8) Yet, we who say we are His children often live in arrogance and rebellion. So many times we have an attitude that demands attention and expects to be served.

Oh, that we would heed this admonition, "Let this mind be in you, which was also in Christ Jesus"! What a difference it will make in our daily lives if we will be willing to let Him teach us to be meek.

- We will have rest in our souls. (Mt. 11:29)
- We will have His help in restoring the fallen. (II Tim. 2:25; Gal. 6:1)
- We will reflect His Spirit. (Gal. 5:22-23; Col. 3:12-13; Eph. 4:1-3)
- We will receive His Word and wisdom. (Jas. 1:21)
- We will reveal His gentleness, His wisdom, His grace, and His glory. (Jas. 3:13; I Pet. 3:4, 15; Jas. 3:13-18; Tit. 3:2-6)

"Blessed are the meek...." (Mt. 5:5)

Assignment:

Meekness is often mischaracterized by the world as weakness. In truth, it is characterized by two great qualities: humility and surrender. The Bible says we are to take His yoke upon us and learn of Him, for He is meek and lowly in heart. Consider your heart. Does it reflect these qualities?

Have you taken His yoke and surrendered your will to His control? Have you chosen to follow His lead, to humbly labor and serve alongside Him?

Study the meekness of Christ. Think on it. How could you learn and practice meekness from His example?

Scripture Writing Challenge

☐ II Tim. 2:24-26   ☐ Mt. 11:29

☐ I Pet. 3:4   ☐ Mt. 21:5

☐ Tit. 3:2   ☐ Gal. 6:1

☐ Eph. 4:1-3   ☐ Gal. 5:22-23

☐ Num. 12:3   ☐ Col. 3:12-13

☐ Isa. 29:19   ☐ Jas. 1:21

Bonus Challenge:

☐ Jas. 3:13-18

☐ Tit. 3:2-6

Niki Lott

LESSON 7

The Benefit of Contentment

This lesson teaches us the "why" of contentment. "…godliness with contentment is great gain." (I Tim. 6:5-7; Pro. 28:16)

As we conclude this study, we find that God tells us why we should seek contentment. We have learned many of the reasons why being discontent is harmful to us, but God also gives us a glimpse into the beauty and benefit of spiritual contentment.

The "gain" spoken of in this verse doesn't refer to some financial or material reward. In fact, it is quite the opposite. We know this for certain, because the Scripture continues, "For we brought nothing into this world, and it is certain we can carry nothing out."

Understanding and practicing God's perspective about "gain" changes us. It frees us from the snare and ensuing bondage of materialism and covetousness.

When we are free from the notion that temporal things can somehow bring us satisfaction, it is then that we gain the joy, the blessings, and the rewards that come from pursuing and enjoying that which is eternal. (II Cor. 4:18; Col. 3:1-3)

Let's take a brief look at God's perspective of gain and some of the lessons He teaches us about what true "gain" is and what it isn't.

What Isn't Gain	What Is Gain
A good education (Phil. 3:4-7)	Wisdom (Pro. 3:13-14; 8:11, 19; 16:16)
Riches without godliness (Ps. 37:16; Pro. 10:2; 11:4; 16:8)	Godliness with contentment (I Tim. 6:5-7)
A good pedigree (Phil. 3:4-7)	A good name (Pro. 22:1)
Religion; morality (Phil. 3:4-7)	The knowledge, fellowship, & power of Christ (Phil. 3:7-10)
Focusing on the temporal, not the eternal (Mt. 16:26; James 4:13)	Dying in Christ (Phil. 1:21)
Earthly possessions with an un-happy family (Pro. 15:27)	A happy home, even with poverty (Pro. 15:16-17; 16:8)
The "great" words of men (II Pet. 2:18-19; Jude 1:16)	The Word of God (Ps. 19:10; 119:72, 127)
Physical health & bodily exercise (Phil. 3:3; I Tim. 4:8)	Spiritual godliness (Phil. 3:7-8; I Tim. 4:8)

True contentment springs from a heart that has set its affection on God.

I ask you once again: Is God enough? (Ps. 73:25-26; Phil. 3:7-10) When we learn that He truly is all we need, we will realize genuine spiritual contentment.

ENOUGH

Frances Ridley Havergal

I am so weak, dear Lord, I cannot stand
One moment without Thee!
But oh! the tenderness of Thine enfolding.
And oh! the faithfulness of Thine upholding,
And oh! the strength of Thy right hand!
That strength is enough for me!

I am so needy, Lord, and yet I know
All fulness dwells in Thee;
And hour by hour that never-failing treasure
Supplies and fills, in overflowing measure,
My least, my greatest need; and so
Thy grace is enough for me!

It is so sweet to trust Thy word alone:
I do not ask to see
The unveiling of Thy purpose, or the shining
Of future light on mysteries untwining:
Thy promise-roll is all my own,—
Thy word is enough for me!

The human heart asks love; but now I know
That my heart hath from Thee
All real, and full, and marvelous affection,
So near, so human; yet divine perfection
Thrills gloriously the mighty glow!
Thy love is enough for me!

There were strange soul-depths, restless, vast, and broad,
Unfathomed as the sea;
An infinite craving for some infinite stilling;
But now Thy perfect love is perfect filling.
Lord Jesus Christ, my Lord, my God,
Thou, Thou art enough for me!

Scripture Writing Challenge

- ☐ Phil. 3:3-7
- ☐ Pro. 28:16
- ☐ Col. 3:1-3
- ☐ II Cor. 4:18
- ☐ Pro. 3:13-14
- ☐ Pro. 8:11, 19
- ☐ Pro. 16:8, 16
- ☐ Ps. 37:16
- ☐ Pro. 10:2
- ☐ Pro. 11:4
- ☐ Pro. 22:1
- ☐ Mt. 16:26
- ☐ Jas. 4:13
- ☐ Phil. 1:21
- ☐ Pro. 15:16-17, 27
- ☐ II Pet. 2:18-19
- ☐ Jude 16
- ☐ Ps. 19:10
- ☐ Ps. 119:72, 127
- ☐ I Tim. 4:8

TEACHING RESOURCES

Niki Lott

Tips for a Bible Teacher

1. Be sure your study centers around the Word of God.

This may seem unnecessary to state, but it is vital. While discussion can be good, the purpose of a Bible study is not to express opinions, but to learn and understand what the mind of God is as expressed in His Word. Although you may not choose to use every listed reference in a class or group setting, seek to always emphasize the Bible as the main focus and resource.

2. Encourage your students to study at home.

This can be done in many ways; however, personal desire to know and understand the Word of God is the greatest motivation.

3. Encourage participation.

Invite students to read Scriptures and to ask questions. As the teacher, be certain that you are able to keep discussions focused on the topic at hand and that you are prepared to handle discussions that can turn into debates or "foolish questions." (II Tim. 2:23; Tit. 3:9)

As much as possible, answer questions with Scripture. If you are uncertain of an answer when a question is asked, don't hesitate to say that you will look into it and get back to them.

If you are asking questions, be sure they are designed to determine if your students understand what is being taught, and to help them think about and gain understanding of what has been taught. Solid Bible teaching should not be designed to "minister questions" that have no answers, or that create confusion or division, but rather to use questions to help people find and grasp the answer.

(I Tim. 6:3-4) (Questions that invite us to examine our own hearts are obviously going to have differing answers.)

Jesus asked many questions in His teachings to cause people to think and to search the Scriptures. He challenged their wrong thinking with questions; however, He did not ask questions for which He did not have the answer. We would do well to follow His example. (Mk. 1:22) This is not to say that we have all the answers! Rather, it is an encouragement for those who are teaching to be well-prepared and to study a topic thoroughly.

4. Pray that the Lord will first teach you what He would have you to teach others.

NOTE: The following outlines/notes are designed to be used along with the preceding book. They are in shortened format. Passages from the study that you may wish to read, but which are not included in the student book, will be in bold with quotation marks beside them. Areas of text that are not in bold will be included in the student books, and any underlined text will be blank in their books, and so will need to be answered in the student book.

Many of the blanks are designed so that the student can fill them in with just their Bible; however, some definitions and quotes will have to be given to them by the teacher. This is to encourage students to attend and participate in the class/Bible study. You may wish to have a completed student book available as a reference for those who may miss a class/study time, so that they can catch up, and have their book completed at the conclusion of the study.

All listed Scripture references for each part are listed at the beginning and will be in the order they are used, unless a reference is repeated. Some "lessons" are longer or shorter than others and are not necessarily going to be completed in one study period.

Finally, many of the illustrations given in the book are personal ones. You are welcome to use them, but feel free to share applicable illustrations of your own instead.

INTRODUCTION
Teacher Notes

The Biblical Definition of Contentment

Scripture References: I Pet. 3:4; Phil. 3:12-14; I Cor. 4:1-2; I Pet. 4:10; Phil. 4:11-13

Opening Statement:

❝ ❞ Consider the following statement, and try to finish it in your mind:

"I would be happy/satisfied/content if _____".

❝ ❞ What is the first thing that filled "the blank" in the previous question? Was it money, a change in your family, relationships, church, status, appearance, or the fulfillment of some dream or ambition? Are you content now? If not, what do you think it would take to make you content? What does it even mean to truly be content?

Contentment is defined in *Strong's Concordance of the Bible* as "to avail, be **satisfactory**, be content, be **enough**, suffice, be sufficient."

Webster's 1828 Dictionary defines the word "content" as "Literally, held, contained within limits; hence, **quiet;** not disturbed; having a mind **at peace**; easy; **satisfied**, so as not to repine, object, or oppose."

Compare to I Peter 3:4: "But let it be the hidden man of the **heart**, in that which is not **corruptible,** even the ornament of a meek and **quiet spirit**, which is in the sight of God of great price."

66 99   **Contentment is a quiet satisfaction, but biblically it goes deeper than that. Before we can understand all that true contentment is, it would benefit us to learn what it is not.**

According to the Bible, spiritual contentment cannot be based on the following:

Status

Stage of Life

Superficial Things

True contentment is not about <u>what</u> we possess outwardly, it is about <u>Who</u> we possess inwardly. Contentment is simply about satisfaction with God and His provision for me.

Spiritual contentment also will not be characterized by these attitudes or attributes:

1. It is not <u>smug.</u>

   -Not <u>conceited</u> (Phil. 3:12) Contentment is not <u>self-important.</u>

   -Not <u>complacent</u> (Phil. 3:14) Contentment is not <u>self-satisfied.</u> (Rev. 3:17)

2. It is not <u>slothful</u> (I Cor. 4:1-2; I Pet. 4:10).

" " **This study is about spiritual contentment - the type of contentment that is not an attribute we naturally possess, yet one that God desires every one of His children to learn. The Holy Spirit inspired Paul to write that he had learned to be content.**

"Not that I speak in respect of want: for <u>I have learned</u>, in whatsoever state I am, therewith to be content. I know both how to be abased, and I know how to abound: every where and in all things <u>I am instructed</u> both to be full and to be hungry, both to abound and to suffer need. I can do all things through Christ which strengtheneth me." (Phil. 4:11-13)

Class Assignment:

Ask your group if they are comfortable sharing areas where they struggle to be content. Take the time to pray together over these specific needs, and ask the Lord to teach you to be content.

Memory Verse: (Phil. 4:11) "Not that I speak in respect of want: for I have learned, in whatsoever state I am, therewith to be content."

LESSON 1
Teacher Notes

The Basis of Contentment

Scripture References: Heb. 13:5; Mt. 6:19-21; Ps. 73:25-26; Phil. 4:19; II Tim. 1:7; Jn. 1:12; 14:27; Phil. 4:6-7; Pro. 22:19-21; Rom. 10:17; Jn. 14:26

66 99 **The first lesson we must learn is the "who" of contentment. The basis of our contentment is not <u>possessions</u> or <u>position,</u> but a <u>Person</u>.**

Who is to be the basis of our contentment? It is <u>God</u>.

Hebrews 13:5 says, "Let your conversation be without covetousness; and <u>be content</u> with <u>such things as ye have</u>: for he hath said, <u>I</u> will <u>never leave</u> thee nor <u>forsake</u> thee."

66 99 **He says that we can be content with <u>what</u> we have because of <u>who</u> He is.**

Question: What do you have that you cannot lose?

(Mt. 6:19-21) "Lay not up for yourselves <u>treasures</u> upon <u>earth</u>, where moth and rust doth <u>corrupt</u>, and where thieves break through and <u>steal</u>: But lay up for yourselves <u>treasures</u> in <u>heaven</u>, where neither moth nor rust doth corrupt, and where thieves do not break through nor steal: For where your <u>treasure</u> is, there will your <u>heart</u> be also."

If we are basing our contentment on <u>temporal</u> things, then our contentment will be <u>temporary</u> at best.

" "   **The key question to this study is this: Is God <u>enough</u>? (Ps. 73:25-26)**

If you know Christ as Savior:

- You have the assurance of His <u>presence.</u> (Heb. 13:5)
- You have the assurance of His <u>provision</u>. (Phil. 4:19)
- You have the assurance of His <u>power</u>. (II Tim. 1:7; Jn. 1:12)
- You have the assurance of His <u>peace</u>. (Jn. 14:27; Phil. 4:6-7)

" "   **If you know the Lord but are still struggling with this area of contentment, don't despair! Remember that Paul said he had "learned to be content."**

Contentment is something we must learn from the Lord.

What are two ways that God teaches us?

1. Through His <u>Word</u> (Pro. 22:19-21; Rom. 10:17)

2. Through His <u>Spirit</u> (Jn. 14:26)

" "   **Are we willing students?**

**"The secret is Christ in me,
not me in a different set of circumstances."**

–Elisabeth Elliott

Class Assignment:

Spend some time thinking about who God is. List some of His attributes.

Here are a few if you need to get them started: Holiness, Love, Mercy, Omnipotence (all-powerful), Omniscience (all-knowing), Omnipresence (present everywhere at all times), Just, Gracious

Memory Verse: (Heb. 13:5) "Let your conversation be without covetousness; and be content with such things as ye have: for he hath said, I will never leave thee nor forsake thee."

Niki Lott

LESSON 2
Teacher Notes

The Basics of Contentment

Scripture References: Heb. 13:5; I Tim. 6:6-8; Ps. 23:1; Ps. 34:10; Mt. 6:24-34; Ps. 68:19

66 99   **In this lesson, we are going to study the "what" of contentment. What physical things does God say that we need to have in order to be content? Let's look to the Word of God.**

Hebrews 13:5 says we are to "…be content with such things as ye have…"

It is put even more plainly and in more basic terms in I Timothy 6:8: "And having food and raiment let us be therewith content."

God says in that verse that there are two earthly basics with which we are to be content:

1. **Food**

2. **Raiment** (clothing)

Read these two verses carefully:

(Psalm 23:1) "The Lord is my shepherd; I shall not want."

(Psalm 34:10) "The young lions do <u>lack,</u> and suffer hunger: but they that seek the Lord shall not <u>want</u> any good thing."

66 99 **There is an important distinction in *having* a "want", and *being* in "want." When we use the word "want" we usually mean a desire, a wish, or even a lust. When the Bible uses the word "want" in these instances, it means a lack or deficiency, to be destitute or in need. There is a big difference in a *lack* and a *lust.* God does not promise to give us every passing fancy or everything we may wish to have. He does assure us that He will meet our needs. Furthermore, the primary needs He promises to meet are spiritual needs, not physical ones.**

66 99 **Here are some tough questions:**

1. If you had nothing but the clothes you are wearing and food to eat, would you be content?

2. Do you think that is even possible?

3. Are you content with the things you currently have?

66 99 **Most of us have far more than what we need, yet we often complain and feel that we are deprived or do not have enough. Sadly, that is ingratitude.**

Read through Matthew 6:24-34. *Encourage ladies to mark the times when it mentions taking thought (there should be five times when it says, "take no thought", "why take ye thought", or something similar).*

Over and over Jesus says, "take no thought" – don't dwell on this, don't fret – about what you will eat or drink or wear. If God can clothe the grass and feed the sparrows, will He not care for you? Then He says, "O ye of little faith." Why did He say this?

"When we are discontent, we are acting on <u>disbelief</u>."

Illustration: The life of George Müller

> **Consider this - Satan's first temptation of mankind in the Garden was for Eve to doubt God's Word and the second was for her to be discontent with God's plan and provision. Eve fell for Satan's temptation. (Gen. 3)**

The account of Eve is also a good reminder that we should be content, not only that we have food and raiment, but with the specific food and raiment God has provided, "...such things as ye have".

Eve's focus on the one thing she could not have instead of all the bounty God had given her opened her mind to temptation and led to her disobedience. Satan often does the same to us. He turns our attention to that ONE THING we don't have and tempts us to be bitter, ungrateful, and even disobedient to God in order to acquire that one thing.

Illustration: Fanny Crosby

Class Assignment:

Ask each person to name one physical "benefit" that God has blessed them with that exceeds food and clothing. There is no doubt each of us could make a very long list, but limit it to one each. Encourage them to take the time throughout the week to write down as many things as they can think of and thank God for each one specifically (they can do this in their student book or a notebook/journal).

Memory Verse: "Blessed be the Lord, who daily loadeth us with benefits, even the God of our salvation. Selah." (Ps. 68:19).

LESSON 3
Teacher Notes

The Boundaries of Contentment

Scripture References: Phil. 4:4, 10-13, 19; Pro. 30:8-9

" " **In this lesson, we learn the "where" of contentment.**

Philippians 4:11 says that Paul had learned "…in <u>whatsoever state</u> <u>I am</u>, therewith to be content."

The word "state" means "<u>condition; circumstance</u>".

The boundaries set forth in this passage are very broad:

- In <u>whatsoever state</u> (condition; circumstance) I am
- <u>Everywhere</u>
- <u>In all things</u>

You may be thinking, "How can I possibly be content in all circumstances, in all places, for all things? That's impossible!" And in our own strength, it is.

Thankfully, the Holy Spirit answers our doubts and deficiencies in verse 13: "I can do <u>all</u> things through <u>Christ</u> which strengtheneth me."

We often use this verse (Phil. 4:13) to apply to different situa-
" " tions, but the context of the Scripture is that of contentment.
We truly cannot be content without God's strength and help
but with His strength, we can be content in any circumstance,
in any place, and in all things.

(Pro. 30:8-9) "Remove far from me vanity and lies: give me neither <u>poverty</u> nor <u>riches</u>; feed me with food convenient for me: Lest I be <u>full</u>, and <u>deny</u> thee, and say, Who is the LORD? Or lest I be <u>poor</u>, and <u>steal</u>, and take the name of my God in <u>vain</u>."

Our human nature tends to be unable to deal with prosperity
" " or poverty. When we have an abundance we are tempted to be
filled with pride and to feel that we don't need the Lord. When
we are in a time of deprivation we are tempted to disobey God and to
blame Him for our troubles.

Paul had learned how to deal with both of these extremes. He states,

"I know both how to be <u>abased</u>, and I know how to <u>abound</u>: <u>every where</u> and in <u>all</u> things I am instructed both to be <u>full</u> and to be <u>hungry</u>, both to <u>abound</u> and to suffer <u>need</u>." (Phil. 4:11-12)

How can we learn to deal with abundance or need with the same grace and peace that sustained Paul? The very next verse gives the answer:

"I can do <u>all</u> things through <u>Christ</u> which strengtheneth me." (Phil. 4:13)

Might I remind you that the Epistle to the Philippians was
" " penned while Paul was in prison? Paul was content in a cell
and Eve was discontent in the Garden of Eden. Why? It wasn't
because of their location or their circumstances. It all hinged on whose
words they believed. Paul believed God and trusted Him. Eve believed
Satan and doubted God.

Illustration: Corrie ten Boom

Class Assignment: Think about people in the Bible who tended to forget God in prosperity, but turned to Him in poverty or trouble. Make a list. Discuss the dangers of pride and prosperity, and the importance of learning faith and contentment in every circumstance of life. (Some examples: the children of Israel, King Solomon, King Asa)

Memory Verses: I know both how to be abased, and I know how to abound: every where and in all things I am instructed both to be full and to be hungry, both to abound and to suffer need. I can do all things through Christ which strengtheneth me." (Phil. 4:12-13)

Niki Lott

LESSON 4
Teacher Notes

The Barrier to Contentment

Scripture References: Heb. 13:5; I Tim. 6:6-10; Eph. 5:5; Col. 3:5; I Cor. 8:4

The Source of Discontent

" " This is a hard lesson because it forces us to take a direct look at the root problem of discontentment. Although it is difficult to face, it is vitally important because we cannot overcome a problem or a sin until we are willing to realize what it truly is, confess it, and ask for God's help. If we get to that point, we can have victory.

Hebrews 13:5 says, "Let your conversation be without <u>covetousness</u>; and be <u>content</u> with such things as ye have: for he hath said, I will never leave thee, nor forsake thee."

" " I Timothy 6:6-10 addresses the need for godliness with contentment and describes that in verses 6-8. It then goes on to describe those who "will be rich," or who desire to be rich, and who love money and what it will give them. It says in verse 10, "...which while some coveted after, they have erred from the faith, and pierced themselves through with many sorrows."

 "   " **God calls discontentment covetousness. Covetousness robs us of contentment. The Lord goes even deeper to be sure that we understand what the root sin of covetousness really is.**

In Ephesians 5:5 we read, "For this ye know, that no whoremonger, nor unclean person, nor covetous man, who is an idolater, hath any inheritance in the kingdom of Christ and of God."

In Colossians 3:5 He says, "Mortify therefore your members which are upon the earth; fornication, uncleanness, inordinate affection, evil concupiscence, and covetousness, which is idolatry:"

 "   " **In both of these passages, we are instructed that covetousness is idolatry. This takes us right back to Lesson 1 and to a painful but vital truth.**

When we are not content with God's provision for us, it is because we love, trust, and desire something other than God. We are idolaters, perhaps not outwardly, but certainly in our hearts.

Finish this statement in your own heart, "I need Jesus and _____".

If there is anything but a period after the word "Jesus" in that sentence, we still have a lot of learning to do. Perhaps there are some secret idols in our hearts. Are we willing to tear them down and lay them at the feet of the Lord Jesus Christ?

 "   " **In Bible days (and still today) people made idols of wood, stone, gold and silver. There is nothing inherently sinful in those objects. They are "nothing." (I Cor. 8:4) The problem is when we elevate those things to a point of worship in our hearts; when we look to them as a source of help, or hope, or comfort, or salvation…or contentment.**

Class Assignment: List some things that are "good things" that can become idols to us – things that we tend to love, trust, or desire more than God.

Memory Verse: "Whom have I in heaven but thee? and there is none upon earth that I desire beside thee." (Ps. 73:25)

The Symptoms of Discontent

When we become covetous, there are certain symptoms that will become evident in our lives over time. It is possible to have some of these symptoms without having all of them, but having any of them should alert us that we are in spiritual danger.

- *__Cravings__* (I Tim. 6:9-10; Josh. 7:21)

" " **When we are covetous, we have the wrong expectations and desires.**

Illustration: Achan

" " **God had forbidden the children of Israel from taking anything from Jericho at that specific time. God wasn't "holding out" on Achan. He was just asking Achan (and the children of Israel) to honor Him first.**

Doesn't He do the same for us? He asks us to bring Him our firstfruits, to honor Him with our substance – those things He has provided for us. Yet aren't we tempted as Achan was to hang on to things for ourselves? Don't we imagine that God is somehow "holding out" on us, keeping us from having what we really want or think we need? Eve fell for the same temptation, and we will as well if we are covetous.

- *__Coldness__* (I Tim. 6:9-10)

" " **When we are covetous, our love for God will grow cold. As we have seen already, covetousness is characterized by having wrong desires, and we desire what we truly love. When our desires shift away from God, our love will also shift.**

"For where your <u>treasure</u> is, there will your <u>heart</u> be also." (Mt. 6:21)

When we do not get what we want, there is a great temptation to grow cold and hard toward God and others. Ice numbs, and sometimes we prefer numbness to pain, but spiritual coldness is terribly dangerous.

" "

Illustration: Those who are dying of hypothermia don't often realize the seriousness of their condition until there is great damage or even death, so coldness of heart can do great damage without us always "feeling" the effects.

Covetousness always comes back to the <u>heart</u>, and our relationship with the <u>Lord</u>. Think of the question Jesus asked Peter three times, "Lovest thou me <u>more</u> than <u>these</u>?" (Jn. 21:15-17)

Do we love God more?

More than what?

More than anything. More than money. More than status. More than security. More than people. More than _____ (you fill in the blank). If there is anything we love and desire more than God, we need to ask the Lord to forgive us and to help us to love Him most.

- *Carnality* (living for the things that please the flesh)

"And he said unto them, Take heed, and <u>beware</u> of covetousness: for a man's life consisteth not in the <u>abundance</u> of the <u>things</u> which he possesseth." (Lk. 12:15)

" " This symptom naturally follows the first two. If our desires are for what will satisfy our flesh and our hearts grow cold toward the Lord, our motives and actions are sure to follow.

Jesus warns us to remember that life isn't about <u>what</u> we possess. No, rather it is about <u>WHO</u> we possess, and Who possesses us.

Jesus followed that warning with the parable about the rich man who laid up much treasure, but wasn't prepared for eternity. (Lk. 12:16-21) In very strong language, God calls this man a fool, and again warns us, "So is he that layeth up treasure for <u>himself</u>, and is not rich toward <u>God</u>." (Lk. 12:21).

" " What are we doing with what we accumulate on this earth and why are we doing it? Are we taking all that God puts into our hands and using it for His glory, or just for our own gain and benefit?

- *Carelessness* (slothfulness)

"The desire of the <u>slothful</u> killeth him; for his hands refuse to labour. He <u>coveteth</u> greedily all the day long: but the righteous <u>giveth</u> and spareth not." (Pro. 21:25-26)

" " Covetous people are often lazy people who feel they are entitled, but have no desire to work for what they desire. It is interesting to note that the Bible doesn't warn of those who are rich, but of "they that will be rich," or those who desire to be rich. It is not money itself, but the love of money, that is the root of all evil (I Tim. 6:8-10).

❝ ❞ **Covetousness has nothing to do with how much or how little we have, but whether we are grateful for, and satisfied with, what God has already given us.**

Proverbs has a great deal to say about the slothful person. We need to ask God to help us to have a content heart, but also a diligent character (Pro. 31:13). We should be willing to work and to be good stewards of what God has entrusted to our care.

The Scripture above (Pro. 21:25-26) contrasts the covetous greed of the slothful with the generosity of the righteous: "...the righteous giveth and spareth not." A good test for our level of contentment vs. covetousness might be how willing we are to give of what we have to others. Are we greedy and stingy, or are we "cheerful givers"?

- *Comparing*

"For we dare not make ourselves of the number, or compare ourselves with some that commend themselves: but they measuring themselves by themselves, and comparing themselves among themselves, are not wise." (II Cor. 10:12)

❝ ❞ **As we have seen, at its root, comparison is dissatisfaction with God, but it often manifests itself as desiring what others have. In that sense, comparison is often both a cause and an effect of covetousness.**

- *Complaining*

"And when the people complained, it displeased the Lord: and the Lord heard it; and his anger was kindled..." (Num. 11:1a)

99

" "

When we are covetous, we will complain about what we don't have rather than being grateful for what we do have. The children of Israel are a tragic example of this symptom of covetousness. We are told in the New Testament that God gave us the accounts of their sin to be examples for us so that we do not do the same things. (I Cor. 10:1-12)

As Jesus said, we need to "take heed, and beware of covetousness." Look for it in your heart and life. If it is there, ask the Lord to help you to remove it. Love Him most. Look to Him as your source of contentment in every area of your life.

Class Assignment:

Consider this list of "symptoms". Can you think of any other Bible characters who struggled with these? How did it affect them spiritually? How did it affect others in their families/churches/communities? (Some people to consider: Solomon, Demas, Nabal, Lot)

☐ *Cravings*

☐ *Coldness*

☐ *Carnality*

☐ *Carelessness*

☐ *Comparing*

☐ *Complaining*

Memory Verse: "Search me, O God, and know my heart: try me, and know my thoughts: And see if there be any wicked way in me, and lead me in the way everlasting." (Ps. 139:23-24).

Niki Lott

LESSON 5
Teacher Notes

The Bewilderment of Contentment

Scripture References: Gal. 2:20; Mt. 20:26-27; II Cor. 12:10; I Cor. 3:18; Mt. 20:16; Rev. 3:17; Phil. 3:10

The Paradox

A paradox is "a tenet contrary to received <u>opinion,</u>" or "a statement that is <u>seemingly</u> contrary or opposed to common sense, and yet is perhaps <u>true</u>" (*Merriam-Webster Dictionary*).

The spiritual life is full of such paradoxes - truths that seem to be contradictory to the natural mind. Here are a few examples:

- To live, we must <u>die</u> (Gal. 2:20).
- To be great, we must be <u>servants</u> (Mt. 20:26-27).
- When we are weak, then we are <u>strong</u> (II Cor. 12:10).
- To become wise, we must become as <u>fools</u> (I Cor. 3:18).
- To be first, we must be <u>last</u> (Mt. 20:16).

> **Spiritual contentment is one such paradox. We discover that when we seek the Lord, our hunger for earthly things lessens. Our hunger and thirst for Him, His attributes, and His work in our life increases.**

The Christian who is self-satisfied may **appear** content.

The church of Laodicea described themselves in this way, "I am <u>rich</u>, and increased with <u>goods</u>, and have <u>need</u> of nothing…" (Rev. 3:17a). They were quite "content" with their condition.

God saw them as spiritually bankrupt.

He said to them, "…and <u>knowest not</u> that thou art wretched, and miserable, and <u>poor</u>, and <u>blind</u>, and naked" (Rev. 3:17b).

> **The Christian who is seeking true contentment has a deep longing to grow in Christ, and to know Him better (Phil. 3:10).**

Contentment is not a satisfaction in <u>ourselves</u>. It is a growing realization that I can find no <u>satisfaction</u> apart from Him and His perfect will.

Class Assignment:

Can you think of any other spiritual paradoxes?

*Some examples:

We walk by faith, not by sight.

We must give to receive.

We must yield to be victorious.

Memory Verse: (Gal. 2:20) "I am crucified with Christ: nevertheless I live; yet not, I, but Christ liveth in me: and the life which I now live in the flesh I live by the faith of the Son of God, who loved me, and gave himself for me."

Scripture References: Ps. 42:1-2; 63:1-3; Job 23:12; Ps. 19:7-10; Pro. 8:11)

<u>The Passion</u>

" " **A Christian who is developing in godly contentment will have a passion to pursue Christ unlike any other. As we stop depending on carnal things to satisfy us, it will cause us to grow more and more dependent on Christ to fill our longings and meet our needs.**

These verses in the Psalms demonstrate this type of passion and desire for God: "As the hart <u>panteth</u> after the water brooks, so panteth my soul after thee, O God. My soul <u>thirsteth</u> for <u>God</u>, for the living God: when shall I come and appear before God?" (Ps. 42:1-2)

"O God, thou art my God; early will I <u>seek</u> thee: my soul <u>thirsteth</u> for thee, my flesh <u>longeth</u> for thee in a dry and thirsty land, where no water is; To see thy power and thy glory, so as I have seen thee in the sanctuary. Because thy loving-kindness is better than <u>life</u>, my lips shall praise thee." (Ps. 63:1-3)

" " **This craving to know and please God more is seen throughout God's Word, and is often compared to hunger and thirst.**

Consider these words of Job: "Neither have I gone back from the commandment of his lips; I have esteemed the <u>words</u> of his mouth more than my <u>necessary</u> food." (Job 23:12)

" " **In this passage, as well as in the Psalms, we see that this passion becomes more important than physical needs. We also see that it becomes more important than typical greed.**

Over and over, the Bible reminds us that God's Word and wisdom are more to be desired than <u>gold</u> and <u>silver</u>. While most of the human race covet temporal things, the child of God who learns contentment in things of this world will learn to desire spiritual and eternal things. (Ps. 19:7-10; Pro. 8:11)

Scripture References: I Tim. 6:3-11; II Pet. 2:1-3

The Parting

66 99 In I Timothy 6, instruction is being given to a young man about discernment and direction in his life and ministry. While the context of this passage is clear, there is also a great deal we can learn about the principles of contentment and the dangers of covetousness.

"If any man teach otherwise, and consent not to <u>wholesome</u> words, even the words of our Lord <u>Jesus</u> <u>Christ</u>, and to the <u>doctrine</u> which is according to godliness; He is <u>proud</u>, knowing nothing, but doting about <u>questions</u> and strifes of words, whereof cometh <u>envy</u>, strife, railings, evil surmisings, Perverse disputings of men of <u>corrupt</u> minds, and destitute of the <u>truth</u>, supposing that <u>gain</u> is <u>godliness</u>: from such <u>withdraw</u> thyself. But <u>godliness</u> with <u>contentment</u> is great <u>gain</u>." (I Tim. 3:3-6)

66 99 In this passage, God warns of those who will not consent to the "words of our Lord Jesus Christ" and "the doctrine which is according to godliness…" Some identifying characteristics of these people are pride, strife (arguing), envy, railings (evil speaking about others, especially God), and evil surmisings (evil and ugly suspicion of others). He goes on to say that they suppose that "gain is godliness." They have it backwards. God's truth is found in verse 6: "But godliness with contentment is great gain."

66 99 Job's three friends made this mistake. While it is true that God had blessed Job, Job's personal and financial losses weren't due to some sin in his life. His friends had bought into the error that "gain is godliness."

God gives a strong warning about false teachers who "…through <u>covetousness</u> shall they with feigned words make <u>merchandise</u> of you: whose <u>judgment</u> now of a long time lingereth not, and their damnation slumbereth not." (II Pet. 2:1-3)

“ ” These people imagine that temporal gain – riches, money, possessions, status – is evidence of godliness. They use our own covetousness to prey on us, to introduce false doctrine, and to draw our hearts away from the Lord. God says, "from such withdraw thyself."

Covetousness is <u>contagious</u> and it <u>corrupts</u>.

“ ” It is often subtle and seductive. Because of this, God cautions us to withdraw ourselves from these types of people. We're not to let them instruct us. We shouldn't expose ourselves to their influence. We don't need to imitate their lives or ministries.

Spiritual <u>contentment</u> requires that we exercise spiritual <u>discernment</u>.

(I Tim. 6:9-10) "They that will be <u>rich</u>…" – those who desire to be rich in the things of this world – "…fall into temptation and a <u>snare</u>, and into many foolish and hurtful <u>lusts</u>, which drown men in destruction and perdition. For the <u>love</u> of money is the root of all evil: which while some <u>coveted</u> after, they have erred from the <u>faith</u>, and pierced themselves through with many sorrows."

God clearly admonishes us to beware of covetousness. He tells us to <u>discern</u> and then to <u>depart</u> from those who are going down this path.

He first says, "from such <u>withdraw</u> thyself" (I Tim. 6:5), and then says, "…<u>flee</u> these things…" (I Tim. 6:11)

We must remember that it is not enough to just separate from the company of those with these attitudes. We must search out and sever those attitudes from our own hearts.

The greatest danger we face is not the temptation from <u>without</u>, but the temptation <u>within</u>.

LESSON 6
Teacher Notes

The Beauty of Contentment

The Pursuit

"…and <u>follow</u> after righteousness, godliness, faith, love, patience, meekness." (I Tim. 6:11)

God doesn't just tell us what to run *from* but also what to run *for*. He tells us as we flee the dangers of covetousness and false doctrine in our lives, we are free to pursue the godly qualities that will bring us true contentment, joy, and blessings in our lives. What are these qualities?

- **Righteousness - our *relationship* with God**

Niki Lott

Scripture References: I Tim. 6:11; Phil. 3:9; Tit. 3:5; Isa. 64:6; Tit. 2:12; II Tim. 3:16; Rom. 4:2-6, 20-25; Isa. 61:10; Rom. 10:3-13, 17; Gal. 2:20-21; Eph. 2:8-10; Rom. 1:17; 8:4-6; 6:9-19; II Tim. 2:22; Job 29:14; Ps. 132:9; Isa. 59:17; Eph. 6:14; 4:25-32; Mt. 5:6

Our righteousness is only and always a result of the work of God in our lives, and the relationship and fellowship we have with Him.

Righteousness is placed <u>inwardly</u> upon us by God <u>at</u> salvation. (II Tim. 3:16; Rom. 4:2-6, 20-25; Isa. 61:10; Rom. 10:3-13, 17; Gal. 2:20-21; Phil. 3:9)

66 99 **We have no righteousness of our own, and yet we can be righteous through faith in Jesus Christ. The Bible says that when we call upon the Lord in faith, this righteousness is "imputed" – reckoned, accounted – to us. His righteousness is placed on our account. Our sin is placed on His account. What an amazing, beautiful, and powerful truth!**

Righteousness does not <u>procure</u> salvation; it is the <u>product</u> of salvation. (Isa. 64:6)

It is not a <u>reason</u> we obtain salvation; it is the <u>result</u> of obtaining salvation.

Righteousness is placed upon us at salvation by God's <u>grace</u> through <u>faith</u> in Jesus Christ. (Eph. 2:8-10)

Righteousness is <u>produced</u> in us by God <u>after</u> salvation.

How can we have righteousness, not only positionally, but practically in our daily lives? God produces the fruit of righteousness in our lives:

- *Through __faith__ in God's Word.* (Phil. 3:9; Rom. 1:17; 10:17)
- *Through yielded __obedience__ to God's Word.* (Rom. 8:4-6; Rom. 6:9-19)

Righteousness should be <u>pursued outwardly</u> for God <u>after</u> salvation. (I Tim. 6:11; II Tim. 2:22)

> **God has given us everything we need to live outwardly what He has made us inwardly. Pursuing a life of righteousness brings glory to God.**

Throughout the Bible, righteousness is compared to clothing.

Name some of these comparisons:

- a <u>robe</u> (Job 29:14; Isa. 61:10)
- a <u>breastplate</u> (Isa. 59:17; Eph. 6:14)
- a <u>priests' garment</u> (Ps. 132:9).

It is to be a visible covering that <u>guards</u> our lives and <u>glorifies</u> the Lord.

> **Ephesians 4 speaks of the difference in the "old man" and the "new man." It describes the contrast between our life of unrighteousness before Christ and the life of righteousness we should live in Christ.**

What are some of the things found in Ephesians 4 that we are to "put off" and "put on" as the children of righteousness?

- We are to "put off" the <u>old</u> man and put on the <u>new</u> man (vs. 22, 24).
- We are to "put away" <u>lying</u> and speak <u>truth</u> (vs. 25).
- We are to be <u>angry</u> and sin <u>not</u> (vs. 26).
- We are not to give <u>place</u> to the <u>devil</u> (vs. 27).
- We are not to <u>steal</u>, but instead to <u>work</u> with our hands that we may <u>give</u> to those in need (vs. 28).
- We are not to let <u>corrupt</u> communication proceed out of our mouth, but instead are to speak words that are <u>good</u> and filled with grace (vs. 29).

- We are not to <u>grieve</u> the Holy Spirit (vs. 30).
- We are to put away <u>bitterness</u>, <u>wrath</u>, <u>anger</u>, <u>clamour</u>, evil <u>speaking</u>, and <u>malice</u>, and instead we are to be <u>kind</u>, <u>tenderhearted</u>, and <u>forgiving</u> (vs. 31-32).

" " **What kind of "clothing" are we putting on today? As God's children, He wants us to live and behave in a way that demonstrates His nature, His mind, and His glory. He desires that we be right with Him and do right to others. Through His grace and power, we can live in a way that is righteous and holy.**

Are we hungry and thirsty for righteousness? Are we pursuing righteousness with the same type of intensity that we would pursue food when we're hungry, a drink when we're thirsty, or riches when we're covetous?

God promises that those who hunger and thirst for righteousness will be <u>filled.</u> (Mt. 5:6)

- **Godliness – Our *reflection* of God**

  Scripture References: I Tim. 2:10; Tit. 2:12; II Cor. 5:15; Rom. 6:10-11; Gal. 2:20

  Godliness is our <u>inward</u> <u>devotion</u> toward God that expresses itself in our <u>outward</u> <u>deeds</u>. It is a <u>piety</u> of <u>heart</u> that is reflected in the <u>purity</u> of our <u>lives</u>. It is the <u>fullness</u> of God's <u>Spirit</u> <u>flowing</u> out in good <u>works</u>. It is the light that <u>shines</u> before men in such a way that while they <u>see</u> our good works, they <u>glorify</u> our great God. (Mt. 5:16)

In order to live in a godly way, we must deny "ungod-
66 99 **liness and worldly lusts." As we have already learned,**
there is always a parting of the ways when we deter-
mine to follow Christ. We cannot live godly and live
worldly at the same time. We must choose to flee one in order to
follow the other. We must learn to die to self, to allow Christ to live
through us, if we are to be like Him. (II Cor. 5:15; Rom. 6:10-11;
Gal. 2:20)

It is easy to think that we cannot truly live a godly life in the corrupt
culture in which we live. It is easy to believe that we must be like the
world in order to win the world. However, neither of those thoughts are
true.

"For the grace of God that bringeth salvation hath appeared to all men,
Teaching us that, denying ungodliness and worldly lusts, we should live
soberly, righteously, and godly, in this present world;" (Tit. 2:11-12)

The grace of God that extends salvation to us also en-
66 99 **ables us to overcome sin, and empowers and educates**
us to "live soberly, righteously, and godly in this pre-
sent world.

Class Assignment:

Godliness is being like God. What are some of the ways that we
can learn to have, and display, the mind of Christ (Phil. 2:1-11)?
Try to name at least five from this passage in Philippians.

- Faith – Our *reliance* upon God

Scripture References: Pro. 3:5-7; Heb. 10:38; 11:1-6; Jas. 1:22; Mk. 11:22; Gal. 3:26; II Tim. 3:15; Rom. 10:17

" " **The life of contentment must be lived by faith. The Christian life begins, continues, and ends with faith. This is not just a generic belief. It is very clear and specific.**

■ Genuine faith is clear in its <u>object</u>.

" " The world likes the idea of faith. "Just believe" and "have faith" are popular mantras, but have little meaning. Faith must have an object. "Just believe" in what or whom? For the Christian, we must be continually aware that it is not enough to just "have faith."

We are tempted to have faith in ourselves, and are constantly encouraged to do so by the world. We can also be tempted to have faith in this world, in power, in money, and so many other unstable things.

We are clearly instructed and often reminded to have faith in <u>God</u>. (Mk. 11:22) We must be careful to keep our faith firmly fixed on the right object – our unchanging <u>Savior</u> and His perfect <u>Word.</u> (Gal. 3:26; II Tim. 3:16; Rom. 10:17)

■ Genuine faith is clear in its <u>obedience</u>.

" " James reminds us that if we hear the Word of God but refuse to obey it, we are deceiving ourselves. (Jas. 1:22) We need to "follow after" obedient faith.

- **Love – Our *revelation* of God to others**

Scripture References: I John 3:18; Jn. 13:34-35; I Jn. 4:19; Mt. 5:44; Rom. 5:10; Rom. 8:35-39; Zeph. 3:17; I Cor. 13; Jn. 17:26; Eph. 4:15; Rom. 5:5; Jn. 14:15; 15:12, 17; II Cor. 5:14; I Thes. 3:12; I Jn. 5:3

66 99 We could spend much time studying what biblical love is and what it isn't. Our world is so confused about love. Sadly, many times, even as children of God, we are also confused about love.

The love we need and should want to follow in our lives is the love of Christ. It is by love that the world will know that we are truly His disciples (Jn. 13:35). If we are to demonstrate this type of love, we must know and understand it. The following thoughts are by no means an exhaustive study of biblical love, but they can help give us a basic understanding and some encouraging reminders.

Christ's love commences. Our love responds.

"We love Him, because He first loved us." (I Jn. 4:19)

66 99 Just as He loved us first, and even when we were His enemies, we should be willing to initiate love (Mt. 5:44; Rom. 5:10).

Christ's love commits. Our love rests. (Rom. 8:35-39; Zeph. 3:17)

66 99 There is an amazing comfort and peace in the knowledge that God's love for us is unshakable. As we learn His love, we are able to offer this same type of steadfast love to others. (I Cor. 13:4-8)

Christ's love conquers. Our love rejoices. (Rom. 8:37; I Cor. 13:8)

66 99 There seems to be a great deal of confusion about this particular point. While it is true that Christ loved us "while we were yet sinners," He loves us enough to free us from that sin if we will turn to Him. His love never approves of sin. He loves us enough to provide a way of escape from sin, not an excuse to remain in it.

His love allows us to conquer <u>fear</u> (I Jn. 4:18), and to conquer sin.

66 99 The love that we can share with others through Christ also has the power to conquer and overcome many obstacles. Genuine, Christlike love cares about people who are sinners (just like we are), but doesn't condone sin.

Genuine love does not rejoice in <u>iniquity</u> or sin, but rejoices in <u>truth</u> (I Cor. 13:6).

Christ's love <u>constrains</u>. Our love <u>relinquishes</u>. (II Cor. 5:14)

66 99 The Bible says that it is His love that constrains us. It compels us and holds us in. It sometimes stops us from doing those things that would go outside the constraints of His love. If we love Him, our love surrenders to that constraint. It is willingly "held in," just as a bride and groom willingly vow to be faithful to one another as long as they live. Their love is gladly constrained to be focused on one single person and object.

When we love Christ as we should, we gladly relinquish our love for the <u>world</u> and the things in it. (I Jn. 2:15)

This love for Him also teaches us to relinquish our selfish desires and rights in order to love those around us. (Rom. 12:10)

Christ's love <u>communicates</u>. Our love <u>reveals</u> (Jn. 17:26; Eph. 4:15).

> **Christ communicates His love to us through His Word and His Spirit. He demonstrated His love by His death for us. (Rom. 5:8; I Jn. 4:10) We reveal our love to Him and to others by what we say, but even more by what we do.**

As I John 3:18 says, "My little children, let us not love in <u>word</u>, neither in <u>tongue</u>; but in <u>deed</u> and in <u>truth</u>."

> **It is important that our actions toward God and toward others are consistent with our words. We need to tell others of God's love for them and of our love for them. We need to then show others by our actions and attitudes that our words are genuine.**

Our <u>words</u> (v. 1), our <u>wisdom</u> (v.2), and even our <u>works</u> (v. 3) are meaningless if they are not motivated by charity (I Cor. 13:1-3).

Christ's love <u>commands</u>. Our love <u>reacts</u>.

"If ye <u>love</u> me, <u>keep</u> my commandments." (Jn. 14:15).

> **These seven brief words concisely and completely summarize how we should react to His love. To react is to respond by action. Because He loves us, He instructs and commands us.**

Our keeping of His commandments is not about somehow <u>earning</u> His love; it is <u>evidence</u> of our love. It is not a means of <u>meriting</u> His love but of <u>measuring</u> ours.

How do we know if we love God? It is not by how we feel or by what we say, but by whether or not we obey His words.

"For this is the <u>love</u> of God, that we keep his <u>commandments</u>: and his commandments are not <u>grievous</u>." (I Jn. 5:3)

The commandment to love God with all that we are is the greatest commandment and should be the greatest aim of our lives. Our love for God should surpass and supersede every other love in our lives. It must be greater than our love for self, our love for our friends, and even our love for our families. This love for God should be the motivating factor in everything we do and say.

" " **In every virtue and fruit God desires to develop in our lives, we grow outwardly in our attitudes and actions toward others as we grow inwardly in our walk with Him. Love is no different.**

How can we best love those around us? By first loving Him that is within us.

As our love grows and matures, it will be evidenced and expressed in our <u>desire</u> to be in His presence, our <u>diligence</u> to keep His commandments, and our <u>deeds</u> before and to others.

This love will flow in spiritual order:

1. It will commence in our <u>spirits</u> as we fellowship consistently with Him.
2. It will continue in our <u>souls</u> as we decide to fully commit to Him.
3. It will be completed in our <u>bodies</u> as we follow His commandments and meet the needs of others.

Class Assignment:

Read I Corinthians 13 as a class. Wherever the word "charity" is used, encourage students to insert their names. This isn't to try to change the Scripture but to help us to realize the personal attitudes and actions that God wants to develop in our lives as we love Him and others.

Challenge Assignment:

Find and read the book, *If,* by Amy Carmichael.

If you do not order a copy to read, search for quotes from it online. Write down at least three quotes that cause you to think about how you can have a more Christlike love. Discuss a few of these in class.

- **Patience – Our _realization_ that God's will is perfect**

Scripture References: James 1:2-4; I Pet. 4:12-13; I Tim. 6:11)

Patience comes as a result of the <u>trying</u>, or testing, of our faith. Patience is a work God does in our lives to <u>mature</u> and complete us. Patience is quietly, calmly <u>enduring</u> hardship and trials. It is being willing to wait <u>cheerfully</u>, without complaint, for God's timing. It is gentle <u>forbearance</u> with those who are not so gentle or forbearing toward us. It is <u>steadfast</u> continuance, despite opposition or even persecution.

Just as we must let God's peace rule in our lives, so we must <u>let</u> His patience <u>work</u> in our lives. (Jas. 1:2-4)

" " **As we do so, we find that the fiery trials He permits are the very things He has chosen to refine and purify us so that we can more fully reflect His working and glory in our lives.** (I Pet. 4:12-13)

" " **Most of us know that we need patience, but we tend to avoid or resist the work of patience in our lives because it is often a painful process. This passage (I Tim. 6:11) teaches us to follow after patience. Desire it. Seek it. Allow it.**

Illustration: Just as you may dread (or even postpone) a needed surgery, but are thankful for the results when the pain and healing are complete, so we often postpone the work of patience, only and always to our own detriment.

Class Assignment:

Many times when we don't "let patience have her perfect work", covetousness can creep in. Read Psalm 37. What are some of the dangers, or demonstrations, of resisting the work of patience?

- **Meekness - our _reaction_ to God and others**

Scripture References: II Tim. 2:24-26; I Pet. 3:4; Tit. 3:2-6; Eph. 4:1-3; Phil. 4:12; II Cor. 10:1; Num. 12:3; Ps. 22:26; 25:9; 37:11; Mt. 5:5; Isa. 29:19; Mt. 11:29; 21:5; Phil. 2:3-8; Gal. 6:1; 5:22-23; Col. 3:12-13; Jas. 1:21; 3:13; 3:13-18)

Meekness is <u>humble</u>, yielded, obedient, and content. It is a defining quality of someone who has yielded <u>control</u> in their life to the Spirit of God and has found Him to be the source of their <u>confidence</u> and their <u>contentment.</u>

Paul said, "I know both how to be abased, and I know how to abound..." (Phil. 4:12) In II Cor. 10:1, he said, "Now I Paul myself beseech you by the <u>meekness</u> and gentleness of Christ, who in presence am base among you..."

" " **Paul had learned the humility required for meekness and contentment. This quality, so perfectly exemplified in our Lord Jesus, is greatly underestimated in our world today. Meekness is one of our greatest needs.**

Why should we want to follow after meekness?

- _Because meek people have yielded control of themselves to God, He often entrusts them with <u>leadership</u>. (Num. 12:3)_
- _Because meek people have yielded their desires to God, He promises they will be <u>satisfied</u>. (Ps. 22:26)_
- _Because meek people view themselves honestly through the mirror of God's Word, they have no illusions about themselves and do not depend on themselves for guidance, so God promises to <u>lead</u> them. (Ps. 25:9)_

- *Because meek people are willing to admit their utter dependence on God and their lack of wisdom, He promises to teach them. (Ps. 25:9)*
- *Because meek people have relinquished their rights on this earth to God, He promises them an inheritance and peace. (Ps. 37:11; Mt. 5:5)*
- *Because meek people are not insistent on living for their own pleasure, God promises to increase their joy. (Isa. 29:19)*

One of the sweetest, yet most rarely talked about attributes of our Lord Jesus Christ is His meekness. He who could rightfully demand the multitudes to worship on their faces came to this earth "meek and lowly in heart." (Mt. 11:29; 21:5; II Cor. 10:1)

❝ ❞ **He was humble. He made Himself of no reputation. He was obedient. He was a servant. (Phil. 2:3-8) Yet, we who say we are His children often live in arrogance and rebellion. So many times we have an attitude that demands attention and expects to be served.**

Oh, that we would heed this admonition, "Let this mind be in you, which was also in Christ Jesus"! (Phil. 2:5) What a difference it will make in our daily lives if we will be willing to let Him teach us to be meek.

- We will have rest in our souls. (Mt. 11:29)
- We will have His help in restoring the fallen. (II Tim. 2:25; Gal. 6:1)
- We will reflect His Spirit. (Gal. 5:22-23; Col. 3:12-13; Eph. 4:1-3)
- We will receive His Word and wisdom. (Jas. 1:21)
- We will reveal His gentleness, His wisdom, His grace, and His glory. (Jas. 3:13; I Pet. 3:4, 15; Jas. 3:13-18; Tit. 3:2-6)

"Blessed are the meek…" (Mt. 5:5)

Memory Verse: (I Tim. 6:11) "But thou, O man of God, flee these things; and follow after righteousness, godliness, faith, love, patience, meekness."

Niki Lott

LESSON 7
Teacher Notes

The Benefit of Contentment

Scripture References: I Tim. 6:5-7; Pro. 28:16; II Cor. 4:18; Col. 3:1-3; Phil. 3:3-7; Pro. 3:13-14; 8:11, 19; 16:16; Ps. 37:16; Pro. 10:2; 11:4; 16:8; Pro. 22:1; Phil. 3:7-10; Mt. 16:26; Jas. 4:13; Phil. 1:21; Pro. 15:16-17, 27; II Pet. 2:18-19; Jude 1:16; Ps. 19:10; 119:72, 127; I Tim. 4:8

This lesson teaches us the "<u>why</u>" of contentment. "But <u>godliness</u> with <u>content-ment</u> is great <u>gain</u>." (I Tim. 6:5-7; Pro. 28:16)

> **❝ ❞** **As we conclude this study, we have learned many reasons why being discontent is harmful to us, but God also gives us a glimpse into the beauty and benefit of spiritual contentment.**

The "gain" spoken of in this verse doesn't refer to some financial or material reward. We know this for certain, because the Scripture says, "For we brought <u>nothing</u> into this world, and it is certain we can carry <u>nothing</u> out." (I Tim. 6:7)

Understanding and practicing God's <u>perspective</u> about "gain" frees us from the snare and ensuing <u>bondage</u> of materialism and <u>covetousness</u>. When we are free from the notion that <u>temporal</u> things can somehow bring us <u>satisfaction</u>, it is then that we gain the joy, the blessings, and the rewards that come from pursuing and enjoying that which is <u>eternal</u>. (II Cor. 4:18; Col. 3:1-3)

Let's take a brief look at God's perspective of gain:

What Isn't Gain	What Is Gain
A good education (Phil. 3:4-7)	Wisdom (Pro. 3:13-14; 8:11, 19; 16:16)
Riches apart from godliness (Ps. 37:16; Pro. 10:2; 11:4; 16:8)	Godliness with contentment (I Tim. 6:5-7)
A good pedigree (Phil. 3:4-7)	A good name (Pro. 22:1)
Religion; morality (Phil. 3:4-7)	The knowledge, fellowship, & power of Christ (Phil. 3:7-10)
Focusing on the temporal, not the eternal (Mt. 16:26; James 4:13)	Dying in Christ (Phil. 1:21)
Earthly possessions with an un-happy family (Pro. 15:27)	A happy home, even with poverty (Pro. 15:16-17; 16:8)
The "great" words of men (II Pet. 2:18-19; Jude 1:16)	The Word of God (Ps. 19:10; 119:72, 127)
Physical health & bodily exercise (Phil. 3:3; I Tim. 4:8)	Spiritual godliness (Phil. 3:7-8; I Tim. 4:8)

True contentment springs from a heart that has set its affection on God (Ps. 73:25-26; Phil. 3:7-10). Is God enough? When we learn that He truly is all we need, we will realize spiritual contentment.

Class Assignment:

Consider the world's perspective of what is "gain" or what is profitable and valuable vs. God's perspective. What are some practical ways that God's perspective on gain should change our lives as believers?

What is the number one takeaway you have from this study on contentment?

Memory Verse: (I Tim. 6:6) "But godliness with contentment is great gain."